HISTORIC HAUNTS
OF THE
LONG BEACH
PENINSULA

SYDNEY STEVENS

Haunted
America

Published by Haunted America
A Division of The History Press
Charleston, SC
www.historypress.com

First published 2021

Front cover: More than a century after her mysterious death, Mrs. Crouch, the preacher's wife, can still be heard singing hymns in the house that was once the parsonage. *Author's collection.*

Back cover: Inez Eugenia Stout, first owner/hostess of the Shelburne Hotel, was known for her meals featuring local ingredients. *PCHS*; lurking beneath the beach sands south of Oysterville, the *Solano* has reappeared periodically since it wrecked in 1907. *EFA.*

Manufactured in the United States

ISBN 9781467147385

Library of Congress Control Number: 2021934141

Notice: The information in this book is true and complete to the best of our knowledge. It is offered without guarantee on the part of the author or The History Press. The author and The History Press disclaim all liability in connection with the use of this book.

For Madam X,
who so generously shared what she saw and heard.

CONTENTS

FOREWORD

Since 1854, when author Sydney Steven's great-grandfather Robert Hamilton Espy cofounded the town of Oysterville on the Long Beach Peninsula in the southwest corner of Washington State, members of the Espy family have been making and recording history and telling tales. Sydney, storyteller extraordinaire in a long line of storytellers, carries on the tradition in *Historic Haunts of the Long Beach Peninsula*, a follow-up to her *Ghost Stories of the Long Beach Peninsula*.

That first ghostly tome generated so much interest that she began to hear from other coastal residents about more ghosts that had been lurking for decades—sometimes generations—in attics, basements, crawl spaces and dark closets. Who better to shine the light on these invisible Long Beach Peninsula inhabitants than Sydney? As you wander these pages, you'll find yourself in the hands of a skilled and reliable guide. Whimsical, humorous and framed in fact, these yarns contain shipwrecks and pets, historic homes and *objets d'art*, as well as idiosyncratic personalities, living and dead. Along this enchanted narrative footpath, you'll learn about local lore, culture and traditions, and you'll be immersed in the unique history of the Pacific Northwest and the Southwest Washington coast.

Often the best stories go untold. But as we say about this fourth-generation member of the Espy pioneer family, "Sydney knows where the bodies are buried." She has unearthed a few of their sagas here, and you'll be delighted that she did.

—CATE GABLE
Columnist, "Coast Chronicles," *Chinook Observer*

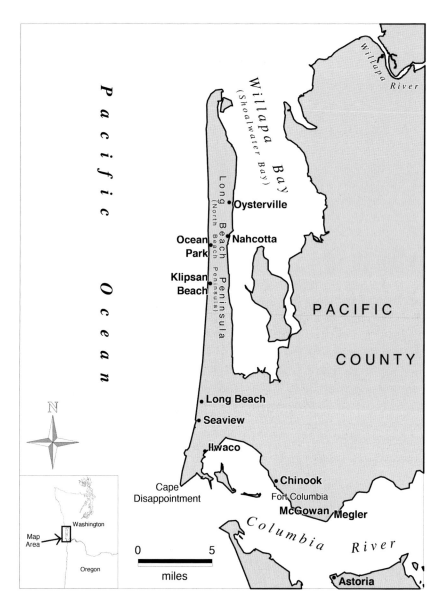

From Chinook to Oysterville, ghosts and their stories flourish in the southwestern corner of Washington State. *Paul E. Staub*.

PREFACE

Storytelling is an art form here on the Long Beach Peninsula. Perhaps that's a carry-over from those long winter nights when it was more enjoyable to spin a good yarn around the woodstove than to try to read by the light of a coal oil lantern. Even today, we old-timers are still repeating the stories that have been told since the earliest days of settlement. That's how we have learned about our history, about the heroes and villains of everyday life and about our oneness with the natural world around us. We've heard about the skeletons in our closets and the ghosts in the unexpected places just out of sight, and we are happy to pass the information along.

Ghosts are more popular these days than they were when I was young. "Popular" in the sense that people talk about them more. I don't mean the ghosts in classic literature like Shakespeare's Banquo or Washington Irving's Headless Horseman. Nor do I mean the sheet-covered kids peering through two big eyeholes as they roam the villages on Halloween. I'm talking here about ghosts that may be unseen companions in ordinary, everyday life. Like skeletons in the family closet, ghosts weren't often spoken about a few generations back.

It may simply be that people are more likely to share all sorts of personal matters now than they once did. It wasn't so long ago, for instance, that phrases such as "my birth mother" or "my sister is trans" were simply not a part of the conversation. Now, there is little that is felt to be inappropriate—even for young ears—and ghosts, like vampires, seem to be all the rage.

Mrs. Crouch (the resident ghost in our home here in Oysterville) notwithstanding, I've always maintained that I don't believe in ghosts—certainly not in the sense that I am frightened of them or feel threatened by their presence. Yes, I have had "experiences" with Mrs. Crouch, all of them inexplicable in any kind of "normal" way. But not one has raised the hackles on the back of my neck. Each encounter has been the sort that is taken with a shrug and an "Oh, for heaven's sake, Mrs. Crouch!" sort of reaction. She definitely feels like a mischievous, yet beloved, member of the household.

In the tradition of my own ancestors and all the other Peninsula pioneers, I can never resist a good story—especially one that involves the history of this southwest corner of Washington State. And if it is a ghost story, all the better! Those included in this book have been calling to me for some time. Several stories are follow-ups to those presented in *Ghost Stories of the Long Beach Peninsula*. Several were prompted by conversations with Madam X. All of them evoke a past that is ever with us here if we but stop to look and listen.

ACKNOWLEDGEMENTS

Some of the ghosts in these pages have been urging me to tell their stories for years. Added to their pleas have been the many residents of the Long Beach Peninsula who have had "a glimmer" or "a feeling" or sometimes "an encounter" and have been generous in sharing their experiences with me. I'd especially like to thank Stephanie Frieze, Cate Gable, Johanna Gustafson, Dave Haeck, Jerri Hawks, Colleen Kelly, Charlotte Killien, Michele and Dave Marshman, Shelly and Doug McSweyn and Tiffany Turner for their firsthand accounts of encounters that are sometimes scary, and sometimes benign, but always mysterious.

For their assistance in providing information and researching historical facts, my thanks go to Joan Mann Alkins, Phil Allen, Ruth Chamberlin, Jerri Hawks, Rachel Katyryniuk, Colleen Kelly, Michael Lemeshko, Rollie Lindstrom, Sharron Goulter Mattson and, most particularly, my "Cuzzin" Ralph Jeffords, whose persistence in pursuing Josiah Crouch's incredible life story is worth a book unto itself!

Images were generously supplied by Adrift Hospitality; Allen Family Collection; Begg Family Photo Collection; California State Archives; David Campiche and Laurie Anderson, Campiche-Anderson Collection; Vicki Carter; Columbia Pacific Heritage Museum (CPHM); Keith Cox of Stony Point Pictures (SPP); Edward S. Curtis; Library of Congress, Prints and Photographs Division, LC-USZ62-90145; Espy Family Archives (EFA); Faye Beaver Collection (FBC); Stephanie Frieze; Cate Gable; Johanna Gustafson; Dave Haeck; *History of Pacific Northwest Oregon and Washington*, vol. 1, 1889

(HPNW); Stacy Katyryniuk; Charlotte Killien; Sharron Goulter Mattson Collection; Ocean Beach Hospital and Medical Clinics Photo Archives (OBHMC); Pacific County Historical Society (PCHS); Deidre Purcell; and the *Seattle Daily Times*. And special thanks to my neighbor Paul Staub, who supplied the perfect map to accompany this book.

INTRODUCTION

Although this book is a continuation of *Ghost Stories of the Long Beach Peninsula*, and although the stories have been calling to me for a long time, I would not have stopped to listen closely had it not been for my late friend "Madam X." When I tell you about her, you will understand why.

Some labeled her a ghostbuster. Or a psychic. Or a spiritualist. But she didn't give herself any title at all. She simply said, "I've always had the gift."

"Always?" I asked.

"Yes. Always. My mother had it, and my grandmother had it too. So do my son and grandson. Five generations."

Had the gift. "Had" as in she had dark hair and a quick smile or even had a good breakfast.

"But," I insisted, "when did you realize that you were…different?" I hesitated to use that descriptor. Maybe she considered the rest of us "different." But she knew what I meant.

"From as far back as I can remember, I always knew when someone was coming to the house or that the telephone was about to ring. I must have been six or seven when I told my mother that my aunt had died. A few minutes later, someone called with the news. That's when my mother said very seriously to me, "Honey, you have a gift; don't waste it.""

MADAM X

Now, almost eight decades later, she asked me not to use her name. "It's all right if you write about me and what I do," she said. "But I'd rather not leave myself open to all the phone calls from the curious and the crazies. If people really need me, they'll find me."

So, I began to think of her as "Madam X." Not that she looked anything like the famous Madam X of John Singer Sargent's portrait—the young, curvaceous Madam Pierre Gautreau who is now and then on display at the Metropolitan Museum of Art in Manhattan. No. Madam X was in her eighties, although her best friend recently told me that no one (including Madam X herself) was certain about her age. "We all know that she was eighty-two for two years in a row. We don't know what other liberties she'd taken."

It was only her bright eyes and interested expression that might have made her stand out in a crowd, and there was a determined air about her—a sense of purpose. But there was no hint at all that she saw more than the rest of us do or that she could take care of problems that even the experts couldn't come to terms with. That's the way she wanted it. Even the story of her life seemed a little jumbled, and Madam X was likely to jump back and forth in the telling.

When she was ten, her mother died, and her father remarried within a few months. "My stepmother didn't like me," she said. "And when she realized that I knew about things before anyone else, she called me a 'she devil' and 'a witch' and beat the holy hell out of me. She was a very strict Catholic and she told me I was sinning. I didn't really have any control over what I knew, and I was too young to understand how to hide my gift. Finally, she dragged me by my hair, threw me into the trunk of the car and drove me up in the hills to a big Catholic building. Maybe it was a convent; I don't know. She said if I didn't shut up, she'd put me in that place and I'd never come out again. Well, I wasn't stupid. I shut up!"

SWEET SIXTEEN

"I got married when I was sixteen," Madam X continued, "and we moved away from the West Coast—far from my father and his wife. By then, I was very good at keeping things to myself, so it was another two years before I

THE WISE WAYS OF MADAM X

"Be respectful. Listen carefully. Offer to help." Those seven words were almost a mantra with Madam X.

"Remember," she told me. "Most of these souls just want to move on, but for one reason or another, they can't. Some feel trapped where they are. Some are afraid. A few are angry or need something to be finished or completed. Each one is different, and each has a story. My job is to help."

She always began with a "drive by" just to get the feel of things. Sometimes all was quiet, but often she felt unrest from the property. Once in a while, she saw figures milling around—sometimes looking at her and signaling.

Always she said a blessing (the Lord's Prayer), and always she asked, "Do you want help?" It was what she saw and felt during this initial reconnaissance that determined what she would need to carry with her on her first encounter with the spirit or spirits she had been asked to contact.

It was usually the following day that she entered the haunted space. With her she carried sage, holy water and a white candle.

- The sage is lit and used for smudging. "Smudging," she told me, "is one way to cleanse a space of negative energy and invite positive energy to connect heaven, earth and humanity."
- The holy water is sprinkled (or spritzed) right, forward and left as she walks through the building. It, too, helps to rid the area of negative energy.
- "The white candle is a repellant," Madam X explained. "The ghosts do not like bright light."

She listens carefully to what is told in answer to her question "Do you want help?" If the negative energy is especially strong, she sprinkles black salt along the threshold and along the window sills. Sometimes called black ritual salt or Witches' Salt, it is made from sea salt, charred herbs and scrapings from a cast-iron skillet.

"Each situation requires its own remedy, and each hapless soul has its own reason for having remained in this world. Usually I can help, but always in a way distinctive to a particular situation—never in the same way twice."

went to see Mrs. LeGrande, a psychic. I went with a group—sort of on a lark—but I found it very interesting. She talked to the rest of the group first and then spoke to me separately. She assured me that I wasn't crazy, and she repeated what my mother had told me years before: 'You have a gift.'"

The rest of Madam X's personal story was complicated and told in a rush with no particular order or sequence. In the years that followed, she had three children; attended Eastern Christian College (now York College) in Valley, Nebraska; was divorced (maybe more than once); and eventually joined a psychic group. "Working with them helped me find expression for everything in my heart, soul and mind." She began to help people with their haunted houses, and as her reputation grew, she was sought after—even by the police to help solve difficult disappearance or murder cases.

She left all that behind, or so she thought, when she came to the Long Beach Peninsula in Southwest Washington in the late 1970s. "But," she told me, "somehow, people who need help find me. I think my mother would approve. I've always tried to use my gift wisely as she instructed so many years ago."

Madam X died a year or two ago, surrounded by those who loved her. There is no need for me to keep her name a secret now, but a promise is a promise. Perhaps you will recognize her in one or two of these ghost stories. Or perhaps she will come to you in a way you wouldn't expect. For certain, she will come with blessings and good wishes. That's just the way she is!

CHAPTER 1

A SPIRITED LINEUP
AT THE LAMPLIGHTER

In Seaview…

I heard about the problems at the Lamplighter shortly after I moved to the Peninsula. There was a new owner, and he got in touch with me and asked for help. "I can't keep my waitresses," he told me. "Louie won't leave them alone."
—Madam X

Of all the old structures said to be haunted on the Long Beach Peninsula, it is the Lamplighter Restaurant in Seaview that should get the "prize" for the sheer numbers of reports and, perhaps, for the persistence of the ghosts themselves. Over the years, there have been countless stories of ghost activities, including (but not limited to) this unlikely cast of characters:

- the old man cook who bangs pots and pans in the restaurant and pinches the young waitresses;
- Lily (some call her Katherine), the barmaid who now hangs out in the women's restroom and was a bit of a floozy, a lady of the night who was murdered and thrown in the cistern; she is beautiful, wears a long Victorian gown and wears her hair in a French twist and decorated with a feather;
- the four-year-old twin girls who burned to death in a fire; they are looking for their mother and are only seen by other children of about the same age;

From 1962 to 2019, the Lamplighter offered food, beverages and even ghostly entertainment to Long Beach Peninsula customers. *Author's collection.*

- a ne'er-do-well guy in plus fours who sits on the bench by the front door waiting for a taxi that never comes;
- David, the young man (eighteen) above the kitchen;
- Eric, a man shot to death in front of the Lamplighter when it was a two-story building.

Although I've gone to the Lamplighter for dinner several times over the last dozen years, I've never been fortunate enough to meet any of these ghostly individuals. However, there has always been a waitress who'd had an "experience" with one of them—especially with the randy old cook. On the other hand, there are waitresses and bartenders who say they've heard the stories but have never had the pleasure of a firsthand, in-the-flesh, face-to-face meeting.

On my first dedicated ghost quest to the Lamplighter, probably in 2010, I went with several friends—one a ghost "believer" only because he had owned a house in nearby Long Beach that had a little girl ghost[*] and he'd had many confrontations with her and her cat. The rest of us were skeptics, but even so, my friend Kay Buesing and I hopefully visited the women's restroom—even hung out there for a while—but to no avail. We also took note of the urn on the mantelpiece with its inscription, "Louie Sloan, 1897–1977," and learned from our waitress that "Louie," one-time owner and cook at the restaurant, was "absolutely!" the handsy, lecherous ghost. "He hasn't been around for a while, now," she said. "Not since that ghostbuster found his ashes and put them in that urn on the mantel."

I tucked that information away in my Lamplighter file, but following that evening, try as I might, I had little luck in learning anything more definitive about Louie or the other Lamplighter ghosts. As for the "ghostbuster" the waitress spoke of, I think I dismissed the idea out of hand. Ghostbusters,

---

[*] From "The Little Girl at the Manor," *Ghost Stories of the Long Beach Peninsula* (The History Press, 2014).

in my mind, were relegated to silly movies that might appeal to middle-school kids.

I turned my attention, instead, to the history of the building itself. I was surprised to find that it had been there only since 1955. However, there had been buildings on the property from "before 1907," according to my friend Joan Mann Alkins, who lives in Seaview, not too far from the Lamplighter. Perhaps the property's history would hint at a story that could explain the Lamplighter's haunted condition.

The Sea View Resort

Seaview was originally conceived as a summer resort community for the Portland, Oregon gentry. The area was platted and named by Jonathan Stout, who had come to the Peninsula in 1860 and had settled first in Oysterville, the county seat. Having tried his hand at a number of occupations, in 1880 he purchased 153.5 acres of ocean beach frontage, first calling it "Stout's" then "Ocean View" then "North Pacific Beach." He finally settled on the name "Sea View," capitalizing on the view from the porch of his hotel Sea View House which faced the never-ending ocean breakers just a block to the west.

JONATHAN L. STOUT

Jonathan Stout had all the mortal makings of a ghost-to-be. Even before arriving in Southwest Washington, he had seemed a bit of a restless spirit. He was born in Ohio in 1824 and moved with his father to Illinois, where he spent his boyhood on the "frontier," as it was known in those days. He learned the cooper's trade, was married and had several children by the time he learned of the California gold strike. By August 1850, he had crossed the plains and reached Placerville, but he had scarcely begun his mining endeavors before he was taken ill. He headed for Oregon, and although he recovered fully in Astoria, he soon returned to Illinois, vowing never to leave home again.

However, by late summer of 1853, he was back in Portland with his wife and family, this time determined never to leave the West Coast again. After a profitable winter, he bought a Donation Land Claim near Oregon City, where he spent the next five years, but when his wife died in 1860, he returned to Astoria on the Columbia River. He soon married Annie Gearhart, twenty-one years his junior, and moved to Oysterville on Shoalwater (now Willapa)* Bay.

For the next twenty years, Stout had what could be called "a checkered career." At various times, he was an oysterman, had his own stage line, worked at his coopering trade, served as justice of the peace, was a saloon keeper and was a customs inspector. One story about the Stouts that endures in my own family concerns the time my great-grandfather R.H. Espy came to the rescue of the second Mrs. Stout and her children during a fierce winter storm. This is the way I've always heard the story told.

It was in the late 1860s that a winter tide lifted the Stout home from its location on the bay bank (the house being about the size of a two-car garage) and carried it seaward in the midst of a driving rain, with Mrs. Stout and three small children trapped inside. Great-Grandpa Espy set aside the accounts on which he was working, unlaced and removed his shoes, pulled on wool socks and gumboots, donned slicker and sou'wester and waded down the flooded lane to his dingy. He upped the anchor, settled the oars in their locks and began to row, using short, even strokes. The wind was intense and the rain heavy, and the house had been bearing toward the bar for nearly an hour. Great-Grandpa, however, followed without hesitation the path of the now retreating tide, glancing over his shoulder at intervals to see where he was going. At last, the Stout house hove dimly into view, already listing to starboard and well down in the water. Overtaking it, he snubbed his boat to a

---

* In the 1890s, South Bend promoters hoped that their newly created town would become the "Baltimore of the Pacific." Fearing that the name "Shoalwater" would discourage sea captains from entering Shoalwater Bay and sailing up the Willapa River to South Bend, they successfully applied for a name change to "Willapa." However, their dream of maritime greatness did not materialize.

porch post, waded over the porch and forced the front door open against the pressure of the water inside. In the living room, he found Mrs. Annie Gearhart Stout in water up to her balloon-like breasts, which she appeared to be using as water wings. She was holding the head of her one-year-old above the surface with one hand and that of her two-year-old with the other. Her three-year-old sat on her shoulders, his hands rooted in her hair.[*] The building had sunk too deep to be towed back home against the tide, so Great-Grandpa used the painter and anchor from his dinghy to moor the house for future salvage and rowed the Stouts back to Oysterville.

J. L. STOUT,
ILWACO, W.T.

Jonathan Stout (1820–1895) did not live long enough to see his Seaview resort become a major vacation settlement at the Peninsula's south end. *HPNW.*

In 1880, Jonathan purchased acreage north of Ilwaco, platted it into lots and named his townsite "Sea View." He promoted it as a resort attraction, opening a large hotel, the Sea View House, which quickly became known for its fashionable amenities, including an elegant dance pavilion, a supply store and stables. But soon Jonathan's life began to suffer serious reverses. In 1887, the Stouts' twenty-seven-year marriage ended in a contentious divorce, and five years later, Stout's hotel was completely destroyed by fire. He died in financial ruin in the mid-1890s. Thus far, however, although more than a century has gone by, there is no evidence that Stout is a restless spirt. It is his son-in-law, Charles Beaver, who has been known to walk the upper halls of the Shelburne Inn just a few blocks north of Stout's erstwhile Sea View House.[†]

---

[*] My friend Faye Beaver, who lived well into her nineties, pointed out years ago that at the time of the floataway, the Stouts were a newly married couple with but one child, Miss Beaver's mother-to-be. She was right, but I tell the story as it was told by my own my mother and by my grandfather before her.

[†] From "The Man Upstairs at the Shelburne," *Ghost Stories of the Long Beach Peninsula.*

THE CHANGING SHORELINE

For tens of thousands of years, the Columbia River has been carrying sand as well as water to the Pacific Ocean. Currents, waves and winds have swept that sand both north and south from the river's mouth, gradually building up beaches, dunes and sandspits at a rate of ten to twenty centimeters per century. When the first explorers arrived on the Peninsula, the long, sandy beach extending north from Cape Disappointment was considerably east of its present location. It was narrow and fairly steep, littered with driftwood and backed by Sitka spruce and shore pine—far different from the beach we see today.

A century and a half later, the situation has changed. In the late nineteenth and early twentieth centuries, jetties were built to the south and north of the Columbia's mouth to deepen and stabilize the river's shipping channel. The jetties also altered the currents along the shoreline, causing vast amounts of sand to be carried landward; along the western edge of the Peninsula, sands began accumulating at a rate of many feet per year. By the end of the twentieth century, as much as three thousand feet of accreted land had been added to the "original" Peninsula that had greeted early explorers and first settlers.

The first cottages and homes in beach communities like Seaview were often built only a few hundred yards from the high tide line of the Pacific, as were the buildings on the property where the Lamplighter now stands. Nowadays, those same buildings and their "descendants" are many blocks from the ocean, and the seashore is completely invisible to them. The accreting sands continue to build dunes, to become established with beach grass and shore pines and to be the focus of great consternation among property owners, lawyers and legislators. But even as these issues are being discussed and, in some cases, litigated, scientists say that a reverse trend is beginning, perhaps due to El Niño events: erosion is now progressing at a rapid rate in some areas north of the Columbia River and presents an ever-changing scenario along the coastline of the Long Beach Peninsula.

The popularity of Stout's Sea View resort grew slowly at first, but in 1888, when the tracks for the new Ilwaco Railroad and Navigation Company brought the train within a few yards of his hotel, the area began to be "discovered." Summer vacationers seeking relief from the hot, inland temperatures flocked to the beach. Some pitched tents among the sandy dunes, while others bought one or more of Stout's fifty-by-one-hundred-foot lots at a cost of $100 each. Although Stout's hotel burned in 1892, and although he never recovered financially, the resort continued to be a great success.

Ghosts usually have a reason for hanging around. Sometimes they don't even know they are dead. My job is to help them get to the other side, but only if that's where they want to be.

—Madam X

Neither the fire that destroyed Stout's hotel nor his death in 1896 put an end to the development of Seaview. It merely put a damper on it. Other promoters followed Stout, and by the turn of the century, the resort was busy again. The *South Bend Journal* estimated that by 1900 there were more than twenty thousand people vacationing there each season.

In no time at all, the Portland social set began building "summer cottages"—some complete with maid's quarters and carriage houses—to which entire households, including horses and milk cows, would "remove" for the summer months. Often, the man of the family stayed behind in Portland to work, arriving on the Saturday evening train for a weekend of rest and relaxation at the beach.

Some of the more enterprising property owners built their places more as cozy resort facilities, maintaining a family atmosphere but geared to the entertainment of summer guests. Frequent advertisements appeared in the Portland newspapers as each summer season approached:

The Hackney Cottage
Seaview, Wash.
Now open for season 1902. On next block
from railroad station. Excellent table
board, with beautiful surroundings. Fine
Surf-bathing. No more attractive place
On beach than the Hackney Cottage.
Mrs. James Hackney
P.O. Ilwaco Wash.

It may be that Mr. and Mrs. James C. Hackney purchased their Seaview property directly from the visionary Mr. Stout himself. By the turn of the

During the early decades of the twentieth century, Hackney Cottage drew vacationers from far-off states and even from foreign countries. *CPHM.*

The Seaview Depot was conveniently located just a block south and east from Hackney Cottage. *EFA.*

century, their "Hackney Cottage" had become a popular destination for summer vacationers throughout Washington, Oregon and beyond. It was situated ideally just a block north and west of the Seaview Depot. There, the little narrow-gauge railroad train stopped twice a day throughout the season. As the only mechanized means of land transport on the

IN THE NEWS

"AMONG THE SUMMER RESORTS"
July 24, 1904
The Morning Astorian

July 23—The rainy days at the beginning of the week discouraged a great many pleasure seekers at the beach and an exodus for distant homes was threatened, but the clouds cleared away just at the time when a few warm days would be most welcome...

An informal musical was given at Hackney Cottage Monday night, at which the following program was rendered:

Solo—Mrs. L.M. Campbell
Duet—Misses Lesser
Piano Solo—Miss Cora Hickey
Mandolin Solo—Mr. D. Pillsbury
Solo—Miss Edna Callipriest

A large watermelon was served by way of refreshments and met with the hearty approval of the guests.

***

A large bonfire was built on the beach, back of the Hackney Cottage, Tuesday evening, in honor of Mr. L.M. Campbell, who left for his home in Boise the following day. The young men of the party told some entertaining stories and sang patriotic songs. When the fire had burned low, the party returned to the house and an informal musical was held. Those present were: Miss Hickey, Miss Peters, Miss Callipriest, Miss Helen Pyle, Miss Caroline Pyle, Mrs. James Hackney, Mr. and Mrs. James C., Mrs. Wenning, Mrs. J.C. Pyle, Miss Nancy Beals, Miss Elizabeth McNerthney, Miss May McNerthney, Miss A. Hackney, Mr. and Mrs. Fred Grant, Mr. and Mrs. Heitkemper, Mr. Rosenfeld, Mr. Al Hackney, Mr. Sloan Hackney and Mr. L.M. Campbell.

***

The guests at Hackney Cottage spent Saturday evening having their futures revealed. Palmistry and card-reading were the means employed and a great many secrets were disclosed, among which was the unannounced engagement of every unmarried person present. The refreshments consisted of a "hand-out" in the kitchen.

Peninsula, its major business from May through September was focused on transporting tourists from the steamer terminus on the north side of the Columbia to destinations all along the twenty-eight-mile-long North Beach Peninsula* and back again.

According to reports in the weekly society sections of Oregon newspapers, the Hackney Cottage did a booming business during the summer months. Often, the list of participants for their various entertainments and fetes included guests from far-off states and even from foreign countries. By 1913, the advertisements were mentioning that the Cottage was "fully electrified," and the entertainments had become increasingly elaborate.

A Death and a Fire

Mention on the social pages came to an abrupt end in 1918, however, when Mrs. Hackney died suddenly and her widowed husband sold the property. The following year, the new owner had recycled the classified ads word for word with the exception of the cottage name, which was now "Seaview Hotel." It continued in business until 1949, when it burned.

Sometimes there's a clear reason for a departed soul to hang around. But not always. It's very satisfying to be of help—especially when it's a child or someone who had an unfortunate time when they were here.

—Madam X

Six years later, Beatty's Restaurant opened on the property, and in 1962, it became the Lamplighter, with owner Louie Sloan doing the cooking. At that time, there were also rooms available for rent in an adjacent, attached building—nothing fancy, but just the ticket for sport fishermen looking for an inexpensive place to bed down between fishing trips.

It wasn't until after Louie died in 1977 that reports of hauntings in the restaurant began. Since the pinching and pot-slamming occurred mainly in the kitchen, it was assumed that Louie was on the rampage, but it wasn't until shortly after Madam X arrived on the Peninsula that answers to the strange happenings at the Lamplighter were made clear.

---

* According to the Geographic Board of Names, the official name of the "sandspit" that stretches north from the mouth of the Columbia River is still "North Beach Peninsula," differentiating it from the beaches to the south of the river. With the arrival of the train in 1889, the possibilities of tourism became apparent, and various booster clubs began a concerted effort to change the name to the Long Beach Peninsula. Thus far, they have been successful only in changing the name in popular parlance.

OH, THAT LOUIE!

Of all the ghosts that roam the Lamplighter, only Louis "Louie" C. Sloan seems to have a traceable history, and even that is somewhat sketchy. That he was a "character," there can be no doubt. According to local lore, he had been a drinkin' man. The former owner of the local auto parts store remembered that Louie would come in from time to time after crashing his car into a ditch when "he'd had a little bit too much." He'd buy the parts he needed to patch up his auto, perhaps ask a little advice and then wouldn't be heard from until "next time."

One of his drinking buddies was Eldred Penttila, owner of the local mortuary. Eldred was fond of telling stories about how the two of them would get to drinking late at night and get a hankering for a good steak. After hours didn't matter. Louie would unlock the Lamplighter, open up the walk-in refrigerator, cut off the "best of the best" from a slab of beef and fire up the grill, and then two friends would have a feast into the wee hours.

If Louie confided in Eldred, the mortician kept his confidences safe. No one knew much about the Lamplighter's owner—where he came from, if he had family, what he had done before he arrived on the Peninsula—until Madam X searched in the mortuary's records. According to the obituary she was able to put together, Louis C. Sloan was eighty years old on December 13, 1977, when he died in Seaview. He was born on January 27, 1897, in Connecticut, was a World War I veteran and had resided in Astoria prior to coming to Seaview "many years ago." He was a retired cook and had operated the Seaview Hotel for a number of years. He was survived by a niece who resided in Connecticut.

Although Madam X found information, she could not find Louie. The records indicated that committal was in Greenwood Cemetery, Astoria, and that Penttila's Chapel by the Sea was in charge of the arrangements. Missing is any record of Louie or Louis C. Sloan having been buried there. "Perhaps," said Madam X, "Louie's niece had intended to get his cremains and something happened."

Apparently, instead of the final arrangements being carried out, Eldred kept Louie's cremains at the mortuary in Long Beach. They were in a storage area where other cremains wait until a friend or a loved one or a history buff (or a Madam X) comes to see to it that they are properly taken care of.

"Not long after I'd moved here, the [then] owner of the Lamplighter got in touch with me," she told me some years later. "I don't know how he knew about me—it happens all the time—but he asked if I could help. He said it was getting so he couldn't keep good waitresses."

So, Madam X and her husband went for dinner. "I met Louie right away," she said. "He was quite a character—nothing shy about him. I asked, as I always do, why he was causing all the disturbances and bothering the workers in the kitchen. He told me that he wanted someone to claim him! He said he had never been put to rest!"

It took some sleuthing, but Madam X finally located Louie's cremains—stored in a box in the back room of Penttila's Mortuary* along with many other unclaimed boxes of cremated remains. Within a few weeks, she and some friends had selected an appropriate urn, arranged for it to be engraved with Louie's name and dates and took it into the Lamplighter for placement on the fireplace mantel in the main dining room. Next to it she placed a small plastic easel on which was printed Louie Sloan's biographical information.

Immediately, the unexplained disturbances in the kitchen stopped. No longer did any of the waitresses or bartenders complain of being pinched. Pots and pans stayed where they belonged. Customers were charmed or, in some cases, bemused by the mantel display in the restaurant. Business picked up. But, in time, so did the unexplained activity in other parts of the Lamplighter.

---

* Unclaimed cremains are apparently not an unusual circumstance. According to Washington State RCW 18.39.175(4): "(2) When cremated human remains have been in the possession of a crematory, funeral establishment, or cemetery for a period of ninety days or more, the entity holding the cremated human remains may arrange for disposition in any legal manner"—subject, of course to specific recordkeeping procedures and proscribed attempts to reach the "authorized agent" or family representative.

Above: As soon as Madam X placed his urn on the Lamplighter's mantelpiece, Louie Sloan stopped his ghostly shenanigans. *Author's collection.*

Left: Despite its benign appearance, according to those who work there, the Lamplighter has been the setting of lively ghost activity for decades. *Author's collection.*

Again, Madam X was called in for a consultation. She found that of the six ghosts still remaining at the Lamplighter, only two wanted to leave. The four-year-old-twins who had apparently died in a fire wanted to be with their mother. Whether or not she had also died in the fire was unclear, Madam X reported, but they seemed to know where she was and were just waiting for someone to help them go to her.

The floozy barmaid, on the other hand, was not interested in leaving the building. Since she had never caused any trouble and, in some ways, was an enhancement to the restaurant's business, the management agreed to let her stay. As far as is known, she is still hanging around the women's restroom. According to Madam X, however, the barmaid did agree to leave—just for a short time, in order to take the twins to the other side to be reunited with their mother. The barmaid, apparently, also thought that the mother had been lost in the fire.

SOME GHOSTS ARE CONTENT

David didn't seem to care where he was as long as it was warm and safe. He eventually moved into the Pilot House Restaurant in Ocean Park. That restaurant has since changed hands, and it's unclear whether or not David is still in the building.

As for the man in plus fours—perhaps an old-time golfer at one of the early Peninsula golf links—Madam X had to confess that she was unsuccessful in making contact. "Perhaps he is happy to wait for the taxi that never comes, revealing himself only now and then without bothering anyone at all."

The Lamplighter ghost stories were told to me the very first time I met Madam X in 2016. She told me she hadn't been back for many years, and we decided that we would like to go for an update. Accordingly, a few nights later, Madam X; Colleen Kelly, the owner of Adelaide's in Ocean Park; my husband, Nyel; and I went out to dinner at the Lamplighter. It felt a little bit like déjà vu.

Again, the waitress eagerly shared her ghost "experiences," especially about Louie, who was up to his old pinching tricks once again. "He doesn't bother me much," she said. "I just tell him to be a gentleman and keep his hands to himself, and usually he does." "I'll have a talk with him before we leave," Madam X said. "He's not keeping his end of the bargain. I may have to take his urn away for a time."

Dinner proceeded uneventfully. Colleen and I went into the ladies' room and hung out, much as Kay and I had done years before. Nothing. Not a glimmer of the floozy. Shortly after we returned to our table, the waitress came with our dessert. When she left, Madam X asked me, "Did you hear that? Did you hear them talking?"

"Who?" I asked. "Who?" Colleen wanted to know. Nyel just looked at the three of us as if we were all a little crazed.

"The ghosts!" said Madam X. "Didn't you hear them? Or at least feel them?" she asked me. "They were right behind your right shoulder, and they were talking to you and to all of us. You *must* have heard something!" she entreated.

I could only shake my head. Whatever gift Madam X was blessed with is not one that I share. Upon questioning, she said that she had had quite a conversation with those ghosts. You could have

I don't often go for a follow-up visit. I like to operate on the basis of trust. If they tell me they'll stay away or if they don't want to leave but promise not to bother anyone, I take them at their word. But once in a while, I'm asked to revisit.

—Madam X

fooled me! I was sitting directly across from her, and she looked intent on the waitress and the pie and ice cream that was being served. Her lips didn't move, and her attention remained on the here and now—or at least that's what the rest of us thought when we talked about it later.

As we left the restaurant, Madam X glanced over at the bench by the front door. We didn't ask if Mr. Plus Fours was there, but we all wondered.

CHAPTER 2

MORE TROUBLE AT THE SHELBURNE

In Seaview…

It stands to reason that a century-old building might have a ghost or two. After all, four or five generations have crossed and re-crossed its threshold during those many years. Factor in that the building has been a hotel from its 1896 beginnings and that hundreds of people have climbed its stairs, walked its halls and spent nights—dreamless or nightmare-filled—in its beds. There was no question in Madam X's mind—no question at all.

Yet when she told me that the Shelburne Inn was "full" of ghosts, I was more skeptical than usual. After all, it wasn't all that many years ago that longtime owner David Campiche had told me that the "psychics from Canada got rid of every single restless spirit in the place. Plus, they identified the main culprit—Charles Beaver himself!"

I have to concede, though, that all of that had been a long time back. Since then, the hotel was purchased by Tiffany and Brady Turner, hoteliers of the first order with establishments on both the Oregon and Washington coasts. They are young and bring new energy to the venerable old building.

The Turners' thoughtful changes have been accomplished with a velvet touch. They have put a great deal of thought into honoring the nineteenth-century character of the building while, at the same time, taking into consideration the amenities expected by their twenty-first-century guests. "We love all the positive energy that we feel in the building," Tiffany said. "That's one of the first things I talked about with Madam X."

The Shelburne Inn as it looks today with the original building to the right and the only remaining additional structure to the left. *Adrift Hospitality.*

CONNECTED THROUGH TIME AND GENERATIONS

Not only is today's Shelburne Inn the oldest continuously operated hostelry in Washington State, but it is also exemplary as a landmark that ties the Peninsula to its historic roots. Local generations both before and after it was constructed are connected and interconnected throughout the towns and villages of the greater Long Beach community.

The Peninsula connections began with Charles Beaver, builder of the original Shelburne Hotel, which now serves as the northernmost wing of the Inn. Charles was educated as an attorney in Meadville, Pennsylvania, and arrived on the Peninsula in 1889. He was admitted to the bar in Washington the following year, but after practicing law for just a year, Beaver decided that a career in the contracting and construction business would be more lucrative.

Meals at the original Shelburne Hotel, prepared by Inez Eugenia Stout Beaver (1860–1930), kept appreciative guests coming back to Seaview year after year. *PCHS.*

Although it is not clear when he and Inez Stout met or when they were married, it seems quite logical that young Charles was influenced in his career change by his father-in-law, Jonathan Stout, who had platted the Seaview Resort in 1880. Indeed, although these days Charles is best known for building the Shelburne in 1896, many of the historic cottages in Seaview were built by him; even today, owners feel a strong connection to the Beaver family.

The Beavers sold their hotel in 1906 and moved to Portland when their children were still young, but pleasant memories and a strong sense of connection brought their daughter Faye (1894–1988) back to the Peninsula when she retired many years later. She never tired of telling about those early years in the hotel and of the roles her parents and grandparents had played in the development of Seaview.

When Portlanders Timothy and Julia Hoare bought the hotel from the Beavers, little did any of them know that the hotel's eventual "Peninsula connection" would be to one of the most influential and far-reaching families of the area. It was the Hoares' daughter Julia who caught the eye of Jack G. Williams of the Ilwaco Williams family. Jack's grandparents were Isaac and MaryAnn Whealdon, who settled in the area that would eventually become Ilwaco in 1858. His parents were L.D. Williams from Wales and Eliza Whealdon Williams, who had grown up in Ilwaco when the area was still called Whealdonsburg after her parents.

Jack Williams courted Julia Hoare in the lobby of the Shelburne, and their descendants claim that the fainting couch still cozied up to the fireplace is where Jack asked Julia to be his wife. Jack, with his larger-than-life sense of humor, was fond of telling folks that when they were married, he had "made an honest woman out of a Hoare." The marriage also ensured that their descendants would one day become participants in the big Williams Family Reunion, which takes place at someone's home on the Peninsula each Labor Day. Now in its eighth decade, the event usually draws upward of one hundred family members from the Peninsula and nearby locations. Every one of them feels a special connection to the Shelburne, and with good reason. It's not only a place to be proud of, but it was also once owned by Williams's forebears.

Someday there may well be Campiche descendants and Turner descendants who feel that same pride of generational ownership. That's just the way it is on the Peninsula when it comes to old structures and landmarks, especially if an ancestor or two is suspected of hanging around for a little haunting now and again.

Meeting the Ghostbuster

"I don't know that we had actually said the words *haunted* or *ghosts* as we worked toward our big opening. We had only little more than a month, and we had a lot to do. For one thing, we cleared all of the furniture out of the second-floor rooms so we could refinish the floors. There were beds and dressers and mirrors all over the place—in the lobby, in the dining room, in the first-floor halls," Tiffany remembered.

About then, she received a call from a friend asking if she'd like to meet a ghostbuster. "She told me that she figured such an old building was bound to have a ghost or two; she thought Brady and I might want to know."

Tiffany was intrigued. "Sure!" she said, although ghosts were the last thing on her mind. "We hadn't run into anything that made us think 'ghost,' but I agreed to meet with her to see what she had to say. As it turned out, I wasn't actually here when she came with the holy water and black salt. But I had done a walk-through of the hotel with her, and her helpers a few days previously. It was a real eye-opener."

Before she even visited that first time, Madam X had done a drive-by, as was her habit before tackling a new situation. "She told me almost as soon as we met for her initial tour of the building that the place was teeming with ghosts,"

Tiffany said. "I guess I was a little surprised at that. As I told her, I knew the building was full of energy, but I wasn't thinking it had to do with ghosts!"

"How do you want me to help you?" Madam X asked. Tiffany told her that she felt a lot of positive energy throughout the Inn, and she didn't want that to be disturbed. "But I asked her to get rid of anything negative. I wanted this to be an upbeat space for everyone—for our employees and for our guests." She continued, "We went everywhere—outside, back to the kitchen and into David's old office, all through the second floor and up into the attic. You have to understand that the place was pretty chaotic. Besides all the stacks of furniture, there were workmen everywhere. But Madam X seemed to tune all of that out as she and her helpers—there were three of them—walked around." Before touring the hotel, itself, the group went out to the south garden. "She asked me what went on out there, and I showed her that there were two ideal spots for small weddings. She talked to someone out there—someone who was unhappy and who the rest of us couldn't see or hear. 'What do you need?' Madam X asked."

"The answer was 'The garden,' Madam X told us." It was an answer that Tiffany was reluctant to accept. "In the end, Madam X showed us a particular tree that she said should never be taken down but said that weddings could take place under it 'there in Annie Mae's Garden' as long as no one faced west. Madam X was very definite about that. That seemed fine; I didn't ask a lot of questions."

The group proceeded through the building. Downstairs, room 16 was a happy place where a couple comes and goes. "Leave them alone when you come back," Tiffany directed. Madam X reported negative energy in the kitchen—perhaps a former cook, she thought—and from a room toward the rear of the hotel. "Charles Beaver's room," she said. Also of concern was a brass bed temporarily located in the dining room. It was full of anger, and perhaps it had belonged to the second owner's wife.

UPSETTING SUGGESTION

One disturbing piece of advice from Madam X was to get rid of the brass bed and, indeed, all of the furniture and mirrors. "We can't possibly do that," Tiffany told her. "They are portals to the other side, you know," Madam X told her. "By keeping all of those that are here, you risk leaving a pathway for the spirits, both good and bad."

Tiffany the hotelier was adamant. "I told her we'd have to take our chances," she said.

At that point in Tiffany's recounting, I very much wished I could have spoken to Madam X before she had ever entered the Shelburne. This is a building I know a great deal about. Not only do I know the former owners, David Campiche and Laurie Anderson, but I also knew the daughter of Charles and Inez Eugenia Stout Beaver, who built the hotel more than a century ago. Besides that, I am a shirttail relative of the granddaughters of Timothy and Julia Hoare, who bought the building in 1906.

The hotel that the Beavers sold to the Hoare family was a fairly simple building. The two-and-a-half-story wood-frame structure was constructed in 1896 as a hotel and boardinghouse. It was built with lumber milled in South Bend, barged to Nahcotta and transported to Seaview by the Ilwaco Railroad. The hotel was located on the block where Sid's Market now stands. It was toward the south end of the parking lot and not all that far from the Seaview Depot.

There were fourteen rooms for permanent and summer boarders, and in addition, the building was spacious enough to accommodate the Beaver

The original Shelburne, across the street from its present location, had fourteen rooms for permanent and summer boarders, plus quarters for the Beaver family. *FBC.*

In 1911, a team of horses pulled the Shelburne Hotel across the street and lined it up with two other buildings. *Campiche-Anderson Collection.*

family, including his wife, Inez, and their two children: Harold, born in 1892, and Faye, born in 1894. Charles named the hotel the Shelburne after a grand hotel in Dublin, Ireland, and he put his wife in charge of running it while he pursued his contracting and building business, primarily in his father-in-law's resort community of Seaview. When he was offered a job with Western Electric Company in Portland in 1906, the Beavers sold the hotel to Timothy and Julia Hoare, restaurateurs in Portland.

Five years later, the Hoares enlarged the hotel by moving the Shelburne across the street to the west side of (now) Pacific Highway, directly north of two other houses they had also purchased. They aligned the three buildings and adjoined them with enclosed hallways. Today, only two of the three structures remain with the original building—the hotel that Charles Beaver built—still the northernmost wing of the Inn. The room in the modern-day Shelburne identified by Madam X as "Charles Beaver's room" is in the wing to the south, directly behind the reception desk. It is perplexing. The room in question is indeed a small apartment, perhaps designed for an early innkeeper, but it is not in Mr. Beaver's part of the hotel, besides which it is highly doubtful that he or Inez ever entered the hotel after selling it.

THE OLDEST PART

On the other hand, under the Campiche stewardship (1977–2018), it was indeed Charles Beaver who was identified by a psychic from Canada. She presumably expelled him from the upper hallways, where he had often roamed, occasionally flirting outrageously with attractive female guests.[*] At the time, innkeeper David said, "That's the area where we frequently heard noises that we could not explain—both in the hallway and on the upper floor room in the northeast corner. Since that's the oldest part of the hotel—the part that Charles Beaver had built—it seemed to make sense and we just accepted the psychic's identification."

Julia Hoare (the second owner's wife) managed the hotel and restaurant on her own from the time her husband died in 1921 until 1939. According to granddaughters JoAnne and Marilyn, their grandmother Julia was "very perfect." JoAnne also said, "To me, she was the greatest woman in the world and could do it all with a happy face. I don't remember that she ever went out. She was always at the hotel."

Julia's room in the hotel, according to her descendants, was room 8 on the second floor. From her window, she could keep an eye on the front door just below. The brass bed that Madam X was concerned about had come out of that very room, but the negative energy emanating from it doesn't fit what any of Julia's descendants knew or have been told about her. So, has some recent occurrence upset her? And what of the Canadian psychic telling David that his ghost troubles were gone?

There also have also been many encounters over the years with "the little girl" and "the old settle" in room 5, both now relocated, apparently, to room 6. In Julia Hoare's old room, too—room 8, just above the front door—there have been many strange and unexplained occurrences, including "the nice man who stayed three days and on the third evening sounded possessed," said one of the publicans. "His voice was completely different and he wasn't at all pleasant like he'd been the first days of his stay. It was really creepy." The brass bed, presumably Julia's, is now in storage, just to be on the safe side, and Madam X took special care to get rid of the negative energy in that room and in the one next door. "It had also been a problem with guests complaining of loud voices and noises— even when the room was vacant," Tiffany explained.

---

[*] From "The Man Upstairs at the Shelburne," *Ghost Stories of the Long Beach Peninsula*.

Heeding Madam X's advice, Julia's brass bed has been removed from the Inn, "at least for the time being," said the Turners. *Adrift Hospitality.*

Guests and staff have reported seeing a little girl dressed in white, swinging her legs as she sits on the edge of this bed-in-the-nook. *Adrift Hospitality.*

After talking with Tiffany, I had an opportunity to speak with David, and I asked him, again, about the psychic who had told him the ghosts were gone. "Not for very long," David said seriously. "I don't think they ever really left." Which made us both wonder if Madam X had managed a more thorough cleansing of the negative energy. Perhaps time will tell.

CHAPTER 3

THE MYSTERIOUS GEORGE JOHNSON HOUSE

In Ocean Park…

The classic Craftsman-style house has graced the northwest corner of Grove and Melrose Streets in Ocean Park for more than a century. Yet it has had few owners in comparison to many of the cottages and homes built on the Peninsula during the same period. Nor have there been many changes to either the exterior or interior. As visitors cross the threshold, they often remark that they feel transported back in time. Even so, only some feel the presence of a ghost.

"Do *you* think there is a ghost in the house?" I asked my friend Charlotte.

"Not really. But I have certainly heard unexplained noises and had some experiences that I can't logically justify. However, my mother was sure there was a ghost. Maybe more than one. But…I don't know…," and her voice trailed off as she thought about it.

Charlotte Killien, owner of the George Johnson House Bed and Breakfast, is a fifth-generation Peninsula resident. Her Chinook tribal roots on her mother's side go back "to time immemorial" she says. "According to Chinook oral history, we have been here since the beginning." The ancient hand-woven cedar baskets and other artifacts displayed in the dining room where we sat give mute testimony to her words.

"But if there are ghosts within these walls, I doubt very much that they have a connection to my family. They were here when my parents purchased the house back in 1970. At least, that's what my mother believed. And

Left: This sign displayed on the front of the George Johnson House is in recognition of its important historic significance. *Author's collection*.

Below: The George Johnson House, a treasured Ocean Park landmark, remains unaltered since its 1913 construction by S.A. Matthews. *Charlotte Killien*.

THOSE ROWDY BAPTISTS!

Ocean Park was platted in 1883 by Isaac Clark, who, with Robert H. Espy, had founded Oysterville nearly three decades prior. Clark, a devoted Methodist, and Espy, a staunch Baptist, had met over a poker game in the winter of 1853, and although their friendship endured, their religious views were always a matter of disagreement.

By the 1870s, Oysterville's busy boomtown atmosphere, with its large transient population and many saloons, had given the town a "sporting atmosphere" that was increasingly uncomfortable for a number of the Methodist families. They were looking for another area in which to hold their summer camp meetings, a popular activity for them during the latter part of the nineteenth century.

Clark suggested to local Methodists and to members of the old Taylor Street Methodist Church in Portland, Oregon (many of whom were already spending their summers on the Peninsula), that the concepts of "camp meeting" and "summer resort" might be combined. The group liked the idea, and an association of twenty ministers and laymen formed a corporation under the laws of the State of Oregon called the Ocean Park Camp Meeting Association of the Methodist Episcopal Church. Clark was asked to plat the new resort.

He located the resort about five miles south of Oysterville, the Pacific County seat. "The Park," as it came to be called, originally encompassed 250 acres. It overlooked the Pacific Ocean on the west and Shoalwater Bay on the east. The plat contained hundreds of lots (the average measuring fifty by one hundred feet), arranged into blocks and streets. In the beginning, leases were given to members of the association, but in 1888, the association began selling deeds.

Each deed contained prohibitions on the use and manufacture of intoxicating drinks, gambling and other immoral practices. Although these restrictions are now

The Oysterville Methodist Church was the first church constructed in Pacific County. It blew down in a 1922 windstorm. *EFA.*

outdated and unenforceable, many deeds still contain those original prohibitions. The first summer cottage (no longer standing) was constructed in 1884 by Mr. and Mrs. Gunstrom, who salvaged their building materials from the beach. Other summer cottages followed, but for a good many years, most members continued to camp in tents.

Among the oldest cottages still standing in Ocean Park from the 1880s are those built by the J.E. Haseltine family, the Lamberson family and the C.W. Gay family. Sometime after the association began selling deeds to its property, the Ocean Park Camp Meeting Association was dissolved. The number of cottages continued to multiply, and so did the number of year-round residents.

Although Ocean Park ceased being a Methodist camp meeting and summer resort site, it has never stopped attracting summer visitors and new residents. With its stores and restaurants and wide paved avenues, the town has become the commercial center of the Peninsula's north end, but the pastoral setting that first attracted early Methodists can still be found among the many narrow residential streets.

many of the visitors to the house have felt 'a presence'—a benevolent presence, according to all accounts."

Benevolent or not, pinpointing the who or the what ghostly source is causing the occasional mystery noises seems difficult. If it is someone associated historically with either the house or the property, the choices are limited indeed. The property was first owned by Edwin Loomis, who lived five miles north in Oysterville and owned a sheep farm five miles to the south, near present-day Klipsan Beach. There is nothing to directly connect Loomis with the house or even with the Ocean Park property, which was apparently one of a number of parcels he owned, perhaps as investments, on the Peninsula.

In 1883, Loomis sold the property to the Methodist Camp Meeting Association. George and Mae Johnson bought it from them thirty years later, in 1913. The house and property remained in the Johnson family until 1969, when the estate of Mae, who was childless and had outlived her husband by some thirty-five years, gifted the house to the Episcopal Diocese of Olympia. A year later, the church sold the house to Neil and Catherine Herrold Troeh, who lived in Seattle but wanted to reestablish a presence on the Peninsula, where Catherine (and her mother before her) had grown up.

Catherine and Neil's daughter Charlotte spent many summers and vacations of her youth in the lovely old house. After her father's death in 1981, her mother began to make fewer and fewer trips to "the beach." It soon became Charlotte's responsibility to oversee any repairs or updates

---

GEORGE C. JOHNSON

George Christian Johnson was born in California on January 26, 1872, and was brought to the North Beach Peninsula when his parents died two years later. Young George was adopted by his uncle and aunt, John C. and Margaret Sullivan Johnson of Oysterville. He went to the Oysterville School, along with the sons and daughters of the first pioneer families of Pacific County, and perhaps for that reason, George had an abiding interest in the pioneer history of the area.

In 1911, George married Mary "Mae" Letscher of New Haven, Connecticut. For a short time before and after his marriage, he co-owned the Johnson-Henry Store in Nahcotta, but when it became necessary to declare bankruptcy, he gave up his merchandising interests and focused on oystering instead. He was well known throughout the county and was frequently asked to speak at public gatherings about the history of the area.

George died in 1934, and from that time forward, Mae lived alone in the house until her own death in 1968. In 1947, she gathered together George's historical addresses and had them published by Frank Turner of the *Tribune* in Ilwaco. Opposite a rare portrait of George, she wrote, "IN MEMORIAM To the memory of my beloved husband and the pioneer people whom he loved, I dedicate this booklet. Mary Letcher Johnson."

The Johnsons had no children. During the many years following George's death, Mae continued to live alone in the house under the watchful eyes of neighbors Marcel and Doug King. Years earlier, George had sold oyster land to Doug, and the two couples had become close friends. In later years, Marcel and Doug's nephew, Rodney King Williams, an elder in St. Peter Episcopal Church in Seaview, told this amazing story about their long friendship:

> *My aunt and uncle, Mr. and Mrs. Douglas King, lived in Ocean Park. She was a Roman Catholic, non-practicing until after my uncle died; he was raised by an Anglican Manxman and a staunch Episcopalian. The Kings owned several hundred acres of oyster land on Willapa Bay, having purchased same from a Mr. and Mrs. Johnson. The two families became very close friends. The Johnsons had no children. Mr. Johnson eventually died, and Douglas and Marcel, my uncle and aunt, became general caretakers of Mrs. Johnson—she was a fair bit older.*
>
> *When Uncle found out that Mrs. Johnson had no will, he helped her to write a proper one for her protection. During the course of many discussions between the three, Mrs. Johnson told my aunt and uncle that she was planning on leaving them $100,000. Uncle said, "No, leave it to St. Peter's." (Mrs. Johnson was also a lifelong Episcopalian.) On a personal note, I have never known anyone to turn down a $100,000 gift. This episode also says something about my aunt and uncle. In a few years, Mrs. Johnson died and actually left $225,000 to St. Peter Episcopal Church.*

that the aging house might need. Over time, the bathrooms and kitchen were modernized, "always in keeping with the age and style of the house," she said, "and with the ultimate goal of opening it as a bed-and-breakfast establishment."

SANDY BEGINNINGS

Like every structure on the Peninsula, the George Johnson House sits on sand. In fact, the entire North Beach Peninsula is composed of sediments brought downstream to the Pacific by the powerful Columbia River and swept northward by prevailing ocean currents. Over time, plants have taken root, bogs have formed in the lower areas and forests of Sitka spruce and Douglas fir have established themselves on drier ground. Basically, though, the Peninsula remains a sandspit, and its stability is tenuous at best.

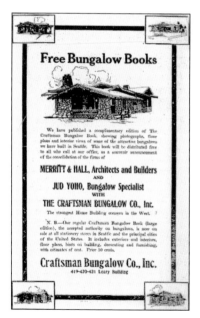

Following the 1909 Yukon Exposition, when Seattle's population tripled from 80,000 to 230,000, affordable Craftsman Bungalows were all the rage. *From the* Seattle Daily Times.

Despite the efforts of nineteenth-century homesteaders and twentieth-century developers to keep the dunes in check with stabilizing grasses, residents know all too well the meaning of "shifting sands."

However, as Mae and George Johnson stood on their recently purchased property in Ocean Park, they found the sand dune underfoot unexpectedly helpful. In 1913, two years after their marriage, they were dreaming about their future and about the house they planned to build. Which way would it face? How would it feel to walk through the rooms? What size would the rooms be?

As they talked, the dune on which they stood became their drawing tablet, and a stick served as the stylus for sketching out their vision. As they planned—rubbing out, re-drawing, imagining as they worked—they came up with the cottage of their dreams. But when they had completed their plan for the first floor, it

S.A. MATTHEWS, MASTER BUILDER

Stephen Adelbert Matthews moved to the Peninsula from his native Maine in 1888. He designed and built a two-story, ten-room frame house in Ocean Park and, in 1891, moved in with his wife and six children. He continued to follow a building career and, by the time of his death in 1934 at age eighty-two, was said to have constructed more than half of the area's early beach cottages.

Matthews was known for his excellent craftsmanship, his sense of humor and the imaginative names he gave his five sons: Sedgewick Adelbert, Valverd Etheridge, Zhetley Vesper, Threllwood Dean and Thedford Leston. Several of the "Matthews boys" also became builders in the Ocean Park area, initially helping their father and learning the trade from him. They continued in his footsteps in the local area—to have a house constructed by one of the Matthews builders is considered a coup, but to own a house by master builder Stephen Adelbert Matthews himself is a genuine triumph!

Master-builder S.A. Matthews's likeness as "The Ancient Mariner" is used as the logo for Pacific County Historical Society's biannual magazine, *Sou'wester. CPHM.*

looked too small, and so they "corrected" their outline in the sand, enlarging their floorplan. Months later, when the structure became a reality, they were both surprised to find that it was bigger than they had imagined—a house, not a cottage!

Among the bits and pieces that are still with the house are its original blueprints by Craftsman Bungalow Company Inc. Architects of Seattle. In 1912, that company had initiated an annual catalogue of perspective drawings and plans that sold for fifty cents. Working drawings and specifications could be purchased for as little as five dollars per set. Whether or not the plans for Mae and George's house were custom drawn for them is unclear. Perhaps they had first purchased the plans and then had drawn them out in the sand to see just how to orient the house. Or perhaps they were trying to better imagine how the traffic flow would be or how they might rearrange the placement of the rooms more to their liking. Actual construction of the house was by local builder S.A. Matthews.

Charlotte remembered that when her folks purchased the house, it matched the original blueprints perfectly. "Underneath one-third of the house was a basement," she began.

The most famous "basement" on the Long Beach Peninsula was built as a result of the Nahcotta School fire in 1936. *EFA.*

"Really? A basement?" I tried not to sound as incredulous as I felt, but Charlotte was shaking her head and laughing. One of those it's-better-to-laugh-than-to-cry sorts of laughs. Everyone over the age of reason knows that you can't have an underground cellar or basement here—not a really-o-truly-o-stand-up-in-it basement, not on our Peninsula. In a place that averages between eighty to one hundred inches of rain per year, the water table is just too high for basements.

The best basement story on the Peninsula has to do with the half-basement under the Ocean Park Grade School. Until 1936, the only school between Oysterville and Long Beach was the Nahcotta School, one mile east of Ocean Park. As increasing numbers of Great Depression refugees arrived on the Peninsula, Ocean Park began changing from a summer vacation spot to a year-round residence for scores of families, and they began to pressure the state for a school. "No money for schools," they were told. "Besides, your kids can walk the mile to Nahcotta School."

The good citizens of Ocean Park made the trek to the state capital in Olympia several times. Miraculously (and mysteriously), the day after returning from their final unsuccessful trip, the Nahcotta School burned. In short order, Works Progress Administration (WPA)* funds were found to finance the Ocean Park School with the proviso that a basement meeting room be built for WPA meetings. Sandspits and water tables were not discussed, and the plans did indeed call for a small basement meeting room. All that could be managed (without risking yearly winter flooding) was a half-basement under the bleachers in the gym. No one remembers now whether it was ever used for anything other than a crawl space—a good area for stacking discarded textbooks and other storage needs. As many an elderly woman now remembers, it was a lovely unseen spot for a hopeful preteen to receive her first-ever kiss.

WEIRD WATER TANK

"Anyway," Charlotte went on, "in the basement there was a huge water tank—at least that's what we thought it was. My dad thought it might have come off a ship. It wasn't attached to anything. In the winter, the basement

---

* The Works Progress Administration (WPA) was an ambitious employment and infrastructure program created by President Roosevelt in 1935, during the bleakest years of the Great Depression. Over its eight years of existence, the WPA put roughly 8.5 million Americans to work and is best remembered for its many public works projects.

would get wetter and wetter—from ground water seepage—and that old water tank would roll around and make a fearful racket. Or that's what I always imagined those noises to be. My mother, though, wasn't so sure.

"There was also an old five-gallon can of boat varnish down there, and it would expand in warm weather and make a loud "*pop-pop*" noise. I have always thought that whoever haunted the house might be into entertaining and healing since it has that vibe…

"As if all the banging and popping wasn't enough," Charlotte laughed, "there were the frogs! Dozens of them down there in the spring, croaking and carrying on to beat the band. Not exactly ghostly—but a little creepy just the same.

"And speaking of creepy. There was the room we called 'The Hook Room.' It's now where the two baths are on the second floor. It was just an unfinished room with a spare bed, shelves and the hooks in the trusses. Lots of them."

"What do you suppose their purpose was?" I asked.

"Who knows? For drying flowers, maybe. Or something to do with drying nets? We never could figure it out.…The most interesting amenity on the original blueprints and in the house, itself, was the half-bath on the second floor," Charlotte said.

A half-bath! In the days when even the crème de la crème on the Peninsula used chamber pots and washbasins and trekked to an outhouse somewhere behind the woodshed, the George Johnson House had a half-bath upstairs! A flush toilet and running water in the sink! Most certainly on the cutting edge.

By 1913, FDR had barely entered politics, and his rural electrification program was twenty years in the future. It is highly doubtful that the Johnsons had a kerosene generator with which to pump water up to their cutting-edge indoor half-bath. It does seem feasible, though, that the water tank in the Johnson basement could have been part of a pressure tank system, perhaps the water storage component.

However it worked, Charlotte is still inclined to believe that the water tank was the source of those noises coming from the basement in the years after her parents purchased the house. "Not a ghost," she said. "But…," said her longtime friend Tom O'Hara, "I'm not so sure."

An Older Woman

"I remember coming to the house back in the late '80s," Tom told me. "For whatever reason, my wife, Jackie, and the kids were coming the next day, so I was alone in the house. Not a problem; I'd stayed there dozens of times and felt totally comfortable and at home. To warm things up, I closed all the doors into the living room, built a fire in the fireplace and was just settling in for a quiet evening when I heard footsteps on the stairs."

"Going up or coming down?" Charlotte asked.

"Definitely going up. I felt sure it was a woman. An older woman."

Tom said he had gone into the hall and looked up the stairs but hadn't seen anyone. "So, I went up, myself, to check it out. Still nothing. But there was a chill wind that seemed to go through the upstairs hall. Nothing else."

"No more footsteps?" I asked.

"No. So, I came back down to the living room and continued my solitary evening. End of story."

"It must be Mae Johnson," Charlotte said. "She's the only elderly woman associated with the house, and she was here on her own for a very long time after George died. And she certainly would have fit the 'benevolent' description that everyone feels."

"We've also had a couple of strange dog things," Charlotte said. Again she grew quiet.

"What? What do you mean 'dog things'?"

As she proceeded to tell me about two unexplained dog reactions, I had the distinct impression that Charlotte might be willing to give more credence to the dogs than to the humans who had said "ghost." It was almost as though she said out loud, "Well, dogs don't dream stuff up. They either hear something or see something or they don't. Not like people and their overactive imaginations." But she only told what had happened, without commentary.

"Early on, I was visiting my folks with a friend and had my Australian Blue Heeler with me. We were chatting in the living room when all of a sudden there was a huge cracking sound. I mean it was *loud*. We all just froze, including the dog. He didn't bark or whine or make any sound at all. His ears were up; his eyes were big and staring into the distance, but not a movement—not a sound. Long after my friend and I returned to our conversation, Whidbey remained on alert. It was definitely strange."

The other incident occurred with a friend's dog. "They, too, were both familiar with the house—had been here many times. But one day when they

This cozy room has been the scene of several "almost" encounters with whoever disturbs the peace and quiet of the George Johnson House. *Charlotte Killien.*

came visiting, the dog began to bark as soon as she stepped into the house. She dashed up the stairs, barking furiously all the way, and then came to a dead stop at the top of the stairway. She continued barking, but she wouldn't move beyond that final step. She was sure something was up there, but for some reason, she wasn't about to go flush it. We heard nothing. Not a thing."

We continued talking about other things. Charlotte told us about repointing the foundation years ago and re-roofing and stripping paint. "Someone had put latex over oil-based paint. What a mess!" she said.

When she began describing the work it took to redo the wallpaper, she said, "Do you know there are thirteen corners in this living room? Thirteen!" I idly wondered if the number thirteen can relate to ghosts and hauntings. I know it's only in western culture that thirteen is associated with bad luck. The Chinese consider it a lucky number. And the house was built in 1913…

But wait! There really is nothing unlucky about this house. It has been well loved since the beginning. And even the ghosts in it (if there are any) seem content. Mostly.

CHAPTER 4

CLOSURE FOR MRS. CROUCH?

Beyond Oysterville…

Author's Note: Of all the ghosts on the Long Beach Peninsula, none seems so compelling as Mrs. Crouch, the preacher's wife. She is the only ghost with whom I've had personal interactions,* and it's probably for that reason that she often has taken center stage in my stories, plays and blog posts. I've talked about her at our summer Vesper services at the Historic Oysterville Church, and she has been the subject in classes I've taught on the history of the North Beach Peninsula. When I give book talks (and never mind that the subject of the book might be far afield from ghosts), there is invariably a question about Mrs. Crouch. The interest prompts me to continue researching the story, but in recent years, I've found very little more about her but a lot more about her husband, Josiah—all thanks to my cousin Ralph Jeffords, "Cuzzin Ralph," who loves to research on the internet. Even before Ancestry.com was available, Ralph was finding out about our family, his friends' families and almost any historic individual who took his fancy. So, of course, I reached out to him early on concerning both Mr. and Mrs. C. The information he has learned about Oysterville's long ago preacher has been simply astounding!

On January 1, 1893, the Baptists of Oysterville, Washington, were at last content. Their just-completed state-of-the-art church was the pride of the community. The old Crellin House across the street was being provided for use as a parsonage through the beneficence

---

* Since 1902, my family—first my grandparents, then my parents, now my husband and myself—have lived in the erstwhile Oysterville Baptist Parsonage. For all those many years, Mrs. Crouch has been a shadowy but beloved member of the household.

Membership in the Oysterville Baptist Church increased from twenty-one to twenty-six during the 1892–93 year when Josiah Crouch served as pastor. *EFA.*

of church deacon Robert Espy. Their newly hired young minister and his family had settled in and were fitting nicely into village life in the small coastal community.

So thankful were the members of the little congregation on that Sunday morning that they scarcely took note of the icy rain or the roar of the frigid north wind outside. For the first time since the Oysterville Baptist Church had been organized back in 1863, there was finally a feeling of physical stability. No longer would the congregation need to meet in members' homes. No longer would they need to wait for an itinerant minister for marrying and burying. No longer would baptisms need to occur in the frigid water of Shoalwater Bay. And if they were feeling just a mite proud, who could possibly blame them?

As Deacon Espy's sixteen-year-old son Harry would write in his diary that night:

> *Sunday, January 1. Rather stormy; cold rain. I went to church both morning and evening at the Baptist church. Rev. Crouch preached two good sermons.*

In a few days, young Harry (who would eventually become my maternal grandfather) returned to school at the Baptist Seminary in Centralia. In Oysterville, the Baptists and their new minister were developing a comfortable relationship. Although the pastor's wife and baby were seldom seen except at church, passersby could often hear Mrs. Crouch singing hymns in her sweet soprano voice as she went about her housework. Josiah's fourteen-year-old brother, Charley, attended eighth grade at the two-story Oysterville schoolhouse, and the senior Mrs. Crouch, the pastor's mother, joined the Village Sewing Bee.

The first glimmer of trouble came the following July, again dutifully (if briefly) reported in Harry's diary:

> *Sunday, July 16. Quite a pleasant day, indeed the sun shone all day. About noon Will Turner came down from Sealand with the news that Mrs. Crouch was drowned in the Willapa* [River] *yesterday.*

> *Thursday, July 27. Still the fine weather continues. Papa went to Sealand where he heard there was a rumor to the effect that Mr. Crouch was suspected of having killed his wife.*

In 1892, the Tom Crellin House served as parsonage for the Josiah Crouch family when he became pastor for the new Oysterville Baptist Church. *EEA.*

The wheels of justice turned slowly but relentlessly. On July 26, a party of law enforcement officers, ministers, doctors and newspaper editors gathered at the Fern Hill Cemetery near South Bend, and the body was exhumed. When the coroner's court convened two days later, the jury "having been duly impaneled and sworn and having heard all the evidence produced thereat" found that "Sarah Angeline Crouch came to her death on the 15th day of July, 1893 by drowning…by some means described by her husband, the only living witness of it as purely accidental."

A few days later, the foreman of the jury, W.H. Woodruff, wrote to prosecuting attorney Marion Egbert, "We were at the time unanimous of our opinion that it would hardly be just to hold him for trial, and were as firmly of opinion that we could not declare him innocent. Hence we aimed to construct our verdict so that the world might know that we entertained doubts."

MIXED FEELINGS IN OYSTERVILLE

If Harry, who was home for the summer, harbored doubts about the preacher, they were not reflected in his diary—at least not explicitly:

> *Sunday, August 6, Osborne* met Mr. Crouch who came in on the late train from Ilwaco all right. There was no cause for uneasiness. He preached two good sermons here but none in Sealand today.*

After Harry and his older brother and sister returned to Centralia for the fall semester, the Oysterville Baptists began to have doubts of their own about Pastor Crouch. At the same time, the sheriff was giving serious thought to signing and issuing a warrant for the preacher's arrest. It is uncertain when Crouch left town, but very probably it was before the Oysterville postmaster received a letter dated November 22, 1893, written by a Mrs. Tillie Crouch claiming that she and Josiah Crouch had been married at St. Joseph, Missouri, in 1885, that he had left her and her (now seven-year-old) daughter in 1888 and that he had subsequently married Sarah Tedder† in 1889 at Gladstone, Arkansas.

---

* Ned Osborne, Oysterville neighbor and Baptist congregation member.

† Mrs. Crouch's maiden name was erroneously identified, initially, as Sarah Angeline Tedden, rather than Tedder—a mistake on my part because of difficulty in reading a longhand notation. The name Tedder is believed to a derivative of the old English name Tudor.

On November 27, Julia Jefferson Espy wrote to her children in Centralia:

> *Mr. Crouch is in Eastern Oregon & is thinking of becoming a General Missionary.*

The following week, Julia again wrote to her children:

As clerk of the Oysterville Baptist Church, Julia may have known more about Crouch than she wrote in letters to her children. *EFA.*

> *You asked about Crouch. We think we have reason to fear we have harbored a wolf in sheep's clothing. His mother rec'd a letter from him yesterday saying he "had learned that a warrant was out for his arrest and while he was not afraid to stand trial, he believed that they wanted to get hold of him to mob him," so he was going to parts unknown.*

In that belief, Crouch was not far off the mark. Just two years previously, a South Bend mob had stormed the county jail at Oysterville and shot and killed two prisoners who were awaiting a new trial for the murder of a young immigrant couple. It must have seemed clear to Josiah Crouch that Oysterville, Pacific County, Washington, was, at least with respect to law and order, still a part of the Wild West.

The following week, Julia wrote again:

> *Your father let Mrs. Crouch have the money to pay her way and she started back to Lincoln, Nebraska Friday. I never saw a more heartbroken woman.*

Years later, when he was an old man, Harry's friend and schoolmate Tommy Nelson summed up Josiah's stay in Oysterville like this:

> *He was a tall, handsome fellow—had an alpaca overcoat. He could sway the women! Why, he baptized one woman who'd been a Catholic all her life! I heard Crouch's wife singing when she was alone and she could sing like a mockingbird. But when a stranger was around, she had nothing to say. My sister went there once. She said she was kind of embarrassed the way Crouch would talk to her and turn his back on his wife. One day he took his wife and baby on a church call up the Willapa and their*

sailboat tipped over. Well, Crouch swum ashore with the baby, but his wife drowned. Well, he was interested in another woman at the time. Well, the sheriff found marks on Mrs. Crouch's neck. Crouch was exonerated, but it got too hot for him and he left town!

News from California

Oysterville's isolation notwithstanding, after Crouch made his hasty departure from the little village, there was occasional news of him. Through their Baptist connections, his troubled congregation learned that he had left Eastern Oregon under a bit of a cloud in mid-December, and shortly thereafter, one of the members received a note from a friend in Los Angeles:

Los Angeles
December 20, 1893

Friend Bub,
I rec'd your welcome letter yesterday morning. I first saw your man here about 10 or 12 days ago or thought it was him at one of the Employment office [sic] here. He looked so seedy and rough that I did not know whether it was he or not but spoke to one of the fellows here about him. And he said that he heard the man say that he was just off the train from Kansas only 2 hours. I saw him yesterday with a small valise. Seemed to be peddling. He was better dressed and looked exactly like Crouch.

At their regular Covenant meeting, the Oyster Baptists deliberated long and hard about their responsibility with regard to the preacher. The December 21, 1893 entry in the clerk's record book stated:

Motion and seconded that the Clerk send notices to the various Baptist Papers of the coast publishing Crouch to the world as an imposter. Motion carried. Motion that the motion be reconsidered and laid over until the regular Covenant Meeting. Motion carried.

Two weeks later, the clerk's entry stated:

Charges of crimes against the Church, his fellow beings, the laws of the land and against God Almighty of Bigamy, obtaining money under false pretenses, and of having left his mother, brother and daughter without means of support and requesting them to go east without it were preferred against Josiah Crouch by R.H. Espy. Motion by Bro. Ireland that Crouch be notified to appear at the next regular meeting and answer to the charges either to defend himself or plead guilty, and that if he did not, he would be expelled. Motion carried.

During the next year, news articles about Crouch appeared fairly regularly in the Southern California newspapers. His reputation was growing, but not in a positive direction. This article in the December 23, 1894 issue of the *Los Angeles Times* was typical:

"REV. JOSIAH CROUCH AGAIN"
The notorious Rev. Josiah Crouch, who operated in this county several months ago, and who was exposed in the columns of The Times showing that he is a convicted criminal and an imposter, as well as being strongly suspected of murdering his wife in Washington about a year ago, is again heard from. As readers of The Times will remember, Crouch pretended some months ago to have become infatuated with a young lady in this county, out in the Trabuco neighborhood, to whom he proposed an elopement, after his exposé in The Times. This proposal was, of course, repelled, and the fellow was ordered to leave the neighborhood, which he did just in time to escape the wrath of a score or more hardy mountaineers who had collected together for the purpose of "sitting" upon his case in an emphatic manner, to say the least. Since that time, Crouch has made himself very scarce until last Tuesday morning, when a brother of the young lady discovered him near their home at the unseemly hour of 4 o'clock. As soon as he was recognized there was a footrace, and, notwithstanding the threats that he had previously made that he would "wade through blood to his chin" to see the "ideal of his heart," he proceeded to demonstrate that he was a sprinter of no mean ability. The brother of the young lady is something of a runner himself, and for fully six miles he gave the pretending "reverend" a race over the mountains and through deep mountain canyons that must have been very interesting, not to say highly disagreeable to him. At last Crouch gave him the slip out in the sagebrush, and the young man returned home to relate what an interesting time he had been having. Then it was discovered that Crouch had left a note at the spring for the young lady, threatening her with

an exposure if she still refused to see him. This note was tied with a piece of ribbon that his address from now on would be Los Angeles. Gracie, his little two-and-one-half-year-old daughter, whom he deserted here is being well-provided for by kindly disposed persons. She has a good home.

It was shortly thereafter, apparently, that Crouch left Southern California for Stockton in the Bay Area. It is not clear whether or not the bits and pieces of information about Crouch that continued to appeared in various California newspapers made their way to Oysterville. Certainly, none was saved for the enlightenment of future historians. As far as is known, the only further news of Crouch was written in a January 1897 letter to the R.H. Espy family from their eldest son, Edwin, by then an attorney with law offices in San Francisco:

You ask about Crouch. He was in for 15 or 20 minutes and talked about people in Washington etc. He is now living in Stockton [California]. *His mother and child are living in Los Angeles. He has married again and I think he said that he had a child.*

Like his younger brother Harry (and most of the Espy men I have known during my own lifetime), Ed was not very forthcoming. The historic record is silent as to whether he was aware of Crouch's newly earned status as an attorney or of the events leading up to his arrest later that same year. From the perspective of our twenty-first-century's information age, ignorance on either of those situations seems somewhat incredible. If he was aware, there is no evidence that he passed the information on to his family or friends in Oysterville.

"ATTORNEY CROUCH; AN ALL-AROUND BAD MAN"
August 21, 1897
Los Angeles Herald

A few weeks ago, J.C. Crouch an attorney, who, after practicing at Stockton had come south to settle in Los Angeles, was arrested on a telegram from the north charging him with grand larceny, and a few days later was taken back to Stockton by an officer sent for that purpose.

Last evening F.W. Matteson, a deputy sheriff of San Joaquin county, returned north, after spending a day or two tracking some of the goods that Crouch is charged with having stolen.

Will White of the sheriff's office assisted in this work, and it is largely through his efforts that his brother deputy from the north was able to recover most of the goods that were shipped from Stockton south.

At the preliminary examination of Crouch, held at Stockton a few days ago, a rather odd state of affairs was uncovered, considering that the defendant is an attorney and a man of more than ordinary intelligence. It appeared that he, with his wife, had been living in a house in close proximity to another one, though not adjoining, both properties being built on one large lot.

Crouch made himself so disagreeable to his neighbors that that fact had a most important influence in determining them to move away. They did so, but left a number of boxes containing the more valuable articles, all ready for forwarding, as well as a quantity of loose pieces of furniture, etc. A few days after this family had moved out, Crouch went to the people having the vacant house to let and represented that he could let it all right if the boxes and furniture were only out of the way.

Probably unaware of Crouch's imprisonment just twenty miles to their west, Ed, Harry and R.H. Espy gathered in East Oakland prior to Harry's November 1897 wedding. *EFA.*

As a way out of the difficulty he consented to store the goods in the basement of his own house, and this was done. But, as it developed later, he had no sooner got the goods under his own control than he proceeded deliberately to dispose of them and appropriate the money to his own use.

He sold a sewing machine in Stockton, shipped some goods to San Francisco, and sold them there, and quite a quantity of goods was forwarded to Los Angeles via Redondo. These last goods were closely watched by the sheriff, and it was when Crouch appeared to take delivery that he was arrested.

Meantime, however, Mrs. had been smart enough to get delivery of some of the things and these she shipped to Bakersfield.

The goods discovered in Los Angeles were scattered all over town. A quantity of silver was found at a livery stable, while some of the goods had been disposed of to second-hand dealers. The total value of the property stolen is estimated at $500 and, on this charge, Crouch was held to answer, his bond being fixed at $5000.

Since then several other complaints have been filed against the sticky-fingered attorney on charges of embezzlement committed when making collections on certain notes.

Conviction and Incarceration

Almost unbelievably, there is no evidence that any information was received by Crouch's former Oysterville neighbors and friends regarding his October 1897 conviction for grand larceny. Nor were they aware of his subsequent incarceration in the California State Prison at San Quentin for a term of three years. Although the available records are silent as to the reason for his early release, Crouch was discharged eight months early on February 19, 1900, perhaps for "good behavior."

Two mug shots, "before" and "after" his years of incarceration, depict two very different aspects of Mr. Crouch. In one he appears neatly turned out and clean, with chin thrust a bit forward—a photograph in which he is seems to be displaying a little "attitude." The second photo pictures him in prison stripes, less kempt, less clean, less self-assured.

Even when being booked into state prison, Crouch seemed unable to tell the truth. "Twenty-eight" he gave as his age. According to his birth certificate registered in Buchanan County, Missouri, he was born in 1866. In 1897, he was, in fact, thirty-one.

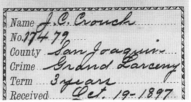

The California Department of Corrections recently released mug shots for Josiah Crouch, taken before and after his October 1897–February 1900 imprisonment at San Quentin Prison. *California State Archives.*

By Any Other Name

By the time of his release from San Quentin, Crouch was going by the initials "J.C." almost exclusively. Perhaps this was to distance himself from his felon status and his disbarment by the State of California. However, in December 1900, just ten months after his release from San Quentin, his name appeared in the *Spokane (WA) Chronicle*. He had been arrested and was waiting to appear before a judge. No further information is available.

He continued in his Spokane law practice without incident until the summer of 1905, when J.C. Crouch was on the move again—first to Southern California, where estranged wife Aurora took him to court demanding child support for their "five-year-old" daughter. It is unclear whether this is the child mentioned by Ed in his 1897 letter. If so, the age is incorrect. Nor is it clear if Aurora also sought (or ever obtained) a divorce, although she did win a fifty-dollar settlement for battery that he promised to pay by noon the following day. Did he? And was he ordered to pay child support as well? Again, the record is silent, at least for now.

The following summer, on June 12, 1908, the *Omaha Daily Bee* announced that on the recommendation of the Bar Commission, one Joseph C. Crouch, having passed the bar examination, was admitted to practice law. From that point forward, the one-time minister Josiah Crouch—aka the convicted felon J.C. Crouch—would forevermore (well, almost always) present himself as "Joseph" and would continue to live in Missouri, first in Kansas City until 1912 and then in St. Louis from 1913 to 1942.

In November 1908 in Holton, Michigan, he wed wife number four, Eva Lois Smith. Information from Ancestry.com indicates that Eva had been married to Thomas Raines Watkins, and together they had had three children. Earlier in 1908, Eva divorced Watkins, married Crouch and then divorced Crouch and remarried Watkins.

Subsequently, "Joseph" Crouch's name could be found listed in the city directories of Kansas City, Missouri (1909–12), and St. Louis, Missouri (1913–40). He did, apparently, pass the Nebraska bar examination in 1909, and he may have practiced legally in other states as well. However, the documentation has yet to show up.

His slight change in name, however, made no substantive change to Crouch's character, at least none that was noticeable, over the remaining thirty-three years of his life. He continued to be connected with nefarious legal proceedings, most notably charges of embezzlement in the late '20s and early '30s involving clients who may have been unable to read and, thus, were easy victims for Crouch's unscrupulous dealings. Finally, in 1933, he was sentenced to one year for embezzlement, according to both the *St. Louis Globe Democrat* and the *Pittsburgh Courier*.

Crouch continued to marry, with or without benefit of divorce. He also continued to practice law, as well as run afoul of it.

A Penchant for Marrying

With regard to his marriages, the newspaper trail was fairly straightforward through 1914, when he won a divorce decree from Della Troyer, to whom he had been married for four years. Della was wife number five, although in later newspaper reports she was named as Crouch's first wife. Between various name changes, age changes and the continuing parade of wives, one wonders if Crouch himself might have been a bit confused.

In 1916, the *St. Louis Post-Dispatch* reported that on August 5 Crouch married Louise M. Cook in St. Louis and that on August 17 he married Elizabeth in Franklin County. Meanwhile, the merry mix-up continued: the *St. Louis Star* reported the marriage of J.C. Crouch and Louise Koch ("Cook"?) on January 26, 1917, in Jefferson City, Missouri. But according to the U.S. Census, by 1920 Crouch was living with Elizabeth in Mobile, Alabama, where he was practicing law. And the beat goes on….

According to information gleaned from Ancestry.com, on June 1, 1924, Joseph C. Crouch, age forty-five, married Elizabeth L. Crouch, age twenty-nine. Oddly, Joseph had once again changed his age. This time, he had subtracted thirteen years from his actual age, perhaps to appear more compatible to the much younger Elizabeth. Apparently, he also claimed that he had only been married once before, although in actual fact, Elizabeth was wife number eight. At least.

"J.C. CROUCH, LAWYER, WEDS SECOND WIFE, DESPITE LOSS OF ANNULMENT SUIT"
June 23, 1924
St. Louis Post-Dispatch

Thrice married, but only twice divorced, Joseph C. Crouch, an attorney of 1411A Market street, gave authorities at Clayton something more to puzzle over by remarrying his second wife there today. The question is, "who's committed bigamy now?"

Crouch divorced his first wife, Della, in 1916. He then married his second wife, Elizabeth. Last June he was granted a divorce from her by Circuit Judge McElhinney on grounds of general indignities. Twenty days later he married Mrs. Bertha Eno, who had just obtained a divorce from her husband, William through Crouch's efforts as her attorney.

From this point the tangle started. It was shown that Eno's name had been forged to papers entering his appearance and he declared that his wife's divorce was illegal. Crouch, hearing of this, asked Judge Wordeman to annul his marriage to Miss Bertha Eno Crouch on the ground that she had committed bigamy. On June 13 the Judge refused to annul the marriage. Crouch had charged that Mrs. Eno forged her husband's name to his statement of appearance. Mrs. Eno-Crouch retorted that she had signed Eno's name, but at the instigation of Crouch.

The Judge said: "If Judge McElhinney, who granted the divorce to Mrs. Eno, had known of her engagement to you at the time, he would not have issued the decree. Had I known of the relationship; I would not have granted you a divorce from Mrs. Elizabeth Crouch. I don't think you did the right thing as a lawyer in not presenting all the facts."

Under the law, as matters stood, Crouch was still married to Mrs. Eno, but her marriage to Crouch was open to attack because of the forgery charge.

To further complicate the situation, Crouch appeared at Clayton today and asked Judge Wordeman to re-marry him to his second wife Elizabeth. He denied he was intending bigamy and contended it was Mrs. Eno-Crouch who had committed bigamy in marrying him with her divorce from William Eno clouded by alleged irregularity. Judge Wordeman declined to decide who was a bigamist.

Crouch's marital status for the next ten years is unclear. Whether the bigamy question was ever settled or what his legal situation was with Mrs. Eno is unknown. Nor is it known whether his marriage to Josephine (aka Jonadia) in 1938 was his tenth, and last, or if there were other marriages in between his marriages to Bertha Eno and Josephine.

By 1938, Joseph Crouch was seventy-two years old. Although he had been sentenced to a year in jail for embezzlement in 1934, there were no follow-up reports to indicate whether or not he actually served the time or if the verdict and sentence had been overturned. By October 1940, Crouch had been appointed to a legal advisory board with two other lawyers—perhaps an indication that after all of his tumultuous years practicing law, he was still thought to be an attorney in good standing.

Josiah/J.C./Joseph Crouch died on October 23, 1942, in St. Louis. He was seventy-six years old, although in his obituary, the *St. Louis Post* stated otherwise:

Josiah C. Crouch Dies at 81. Josiah C. Crouch, an attorney, was found dead in bed at his home, 1634 Park Avenue, yesterday by his wife, Mrs. Josephine Crouch. He was 81 years old, and death was attributed to infirmities of age. He had been under the care of a physician for several months.

Crouch appears to have died a pauper, being buried in a potters' field and leaving Josephine with no visible means of support.

There may well be more to Crouch's story. Although the record shows that his eldest daughter (born to first wife Tillie Lindgren Crouch), Mayme, died in 1959 in Los Angeles, she was apparently unmarried and died without children. Of Sarah's daughter Gracie, there is no information beyond several

JOSIAH CROUCH TIMELINE, 1866–1942

Perhaps Josiah Crouch's greatest success in life was in keeping his name before the public, whether or not he wanted to. There are scores of newspaper accounts in dozens of cities telling of his shady shenanigans. Reports from Arkansas, Washington, Oregon, California, Missouri, Kansas, Nebraska and Pennsylvania followed his nefarious dealings, mostly with regard to his numerous wives and confused domestic arrangements. More recently, he shows up in various Ancestry.com documents, often in conflicting reports. The following timeline, though not necessarily complete, may be of assistance to curious readers:

1866, Josiah Columbus Crouch, born in Buchanan County, Missouri
1885, August, Marriage no. 1, Tillie Lindgren, St. Joseph, Missouri
1889, December, Marriage no. 2, Sarah Angeline Tedder, Garland County, Arkansas
1894, Marriage no. 3, Aurora Nelson, Los Angeles, California
1908, November, Marriage no. 4, Eva Lois Smith, Holton, Missouri
1910, January, Marriage no. 5, Della Troyer, Kansas City, Missouri
1910, January, Marriage no. 6, Elizabeth L., St. Louis, Missouri
1908, Marriage no. 7, Eva Lois Smith Watkins, Holton, Missouri
1916, Marriage no. 8, Louise M. Koch (or Cook), St. Louis, Missouri
1917, Marriage no. 9, January, Louise M. Koch (or Cook), Missouri County
1923, Marriage no. 10, Bertha Eno, St. Louis, Missouri
1924, June 1, Marriage no. 11, Elizabeth L. Crouch, St. Louis, Missouri
1924, June, Marriage no. 12, Bertha Eno, St. Louis, Missouri
1938, Marriage no. 13, Josephine (Jonadia)

Although it appears that Crouch was married (at least) thirteen times, it must be pointed out that he seems to have been married on two different occasions to Eva Lois Smith Watkins, to Elizabeth L. and to Bertha Eno, unless of course the records were confused (which seems entirely possible).

As for deaths, annulments, divorces or other endings to Crouch's marriages, the record is even less clear. His 1889 marriage to Sarah, of course, ended with her death in 1894. Subsequently, the following endings (at least for a time) appear to have taken place:

1908, Eva Smith Watkins apparently divorced a Mr. Watkins in 1908 in order to marry Crouch and then divorced Crouch to remarry Watkins

1916, Crouch divorced Della Troyer

1923, Crouch divorced Elizabeth L.

The final tally, at least as of this writing, seems to be thirteen marriages, two of which were canceled by death (Sarah's and his own) and three by divorce, leaving eight in an unresolved state. Perhaps Larry Murante said it all in his "Ballad of Mrs. Crouch": "He was not a righteous man."

1894 *Los Angeles Times* articles telling that after Crouch had established himself in the vicinity of El Toro, where he was holding revival services and "winning the confidence of Mrs. Shaw and her daughter, whom he proposed to marry, he brought little Gracie to Los Angeles to their home, where evidently he intended to leave her"; later, there was the report of Gracie being cared for by "kindly disposed persons" in the L.A. area.

So, unless the ghost of Sarah Crouch reveals what happened on the Willapa River back in June 1893, or unless Crouch himself left a diary or other firsthand account about his 1892–93 stay at the Baptist Parsonage in Oysterville, we are unlikely to settle the mystery of Sarah Crouch's drowning. Each person who hears Reverend Crouch's story will need to decide his guilt or innocence on his or her own.

CHAPTER 5

THE GHOST AT CROW COTTAGE

In Ilwaco…

The tidy little house sits on the northeast corner of Elizabeth and Spruce Streets in Ilwaco, looking for all the world like the honeymoon cottage or the starter house we all dreamed about once upon a time. And in a way, owners Stephanie Frieze and Dave Haeck had a similar dream when they married in 1990.

Not that they thought of it as a honeymoon cottage, and it was certainly not a starter house either. Theirs is a midlife marriage, and Dave already had a house that they planned to move into with Stephanie's twenty-one-year-old daughter, three sons (a sixth grader, a sophomore and a junior in high school) and her widowed mother. They would be moving up to the Puget Sound area, and the "beach house" was Dave's promise to Stephanie that one day they would retire to Ilwaco and the Long Beach Peninsula. She had a long history at the beach and wanted it to continue.

"Little did I think that by the time we were ready to retire, getting up those steep, narrow steps on a daily basis would be too much for me," Stephanie said, laughing. Nor did she anticipate that daughter Amy Casey would have moved into the only downstairs bedroom. Or that her grandchildren would all be four hours north in the Tacoma area and that she, the participatory grandmother, would want to be nearby when her great retirement day finally arrived. "It's hard to see into the future," said Stephanie, "and sometimes it's even harder when you get there and see it up close and personal."

Crow Cottage in Ilwaco is the picture-perfect beach getaway destination. "The ghostly resident just adds interest to our visits," said family members. *Stephanie Frieze.*

They named it "Crow Cottage" because there were ("and still are!") always so many crows outside—on the roof, on the fence, in the yard. "It was painted yellow when we bought it, but even so, multiple old folks stopped by at first to tell us that it had always been red. In the old days. Maybe we should have called it 'The Red House,'" she laughed.

Over the years, Stephanie and Dave have made many repairs and improvements. They've re-roofed, repainted and re-sided. They've put in five new windows, and they took out five layers of linoleum from the kitchen. But the house has always kept its original character as far as Stephanie and Dave can determine. Much of what they know about its history comes from friendly neighbors and Stephanie's own longtime knowledge of the area and its history.

"Jon Kaino's family has been here for generations. He was the realtor who sold the cottage to us, and according to him, it was built in 1881 in the area of Ilwaco once known as Whealdonsburg."

PENINSULA ROOTS

"Our family goes back to my mother's grandparents, Royal and Amanda Austin," said Stephanie. "They would come from Ocosta, up on the coast in Grays Harbor County, and rent a house in Ocean Park. My mother said Amanda rode the stagecoach on the beach to visit her friends the Loomises. There's some mystery surrounding my grandmother's birth...but that's another story."

In the 1940s, Stephanie's mother's parents bought a beach house in Seaview. The house was at Thirty-Second and K Place and had been built in 1891. "My grandparents were political animals—Grandpa had been in the state legislature, as had been his father and his father-in-law, all Republicans. When the Republicans held their national

In schoolgirl handwriting on the back of Stephanie's picture is written, "The beach is in my blood. And in my eye." *Frieze Family Album.*

convention at the Cow Palace in San Francisco in August 1956," Stephanie remembered, "Grandma loved the name and she greatly admired Eisenhower, so she named their beach house 'The Cow Palace' and her cocker spaniel 'Ike.' My father painted a Cow Palace sign that was red on white that stood out against the weathered shingles. It was good to have names on houses in those days. Daddy hung it above the south side of the porch facing Thirty-Second Street. It was a double lot, and everyone parked on that side of the house, remembering Grandpa's admonishment not to park over the cesspool."

Stephanie's fondest memories of those times are of "hanging out with my dad, flying kites, walking to Sugarman's Store with him for comic books (did you know that Joe Sugarman kept penny candy on the counter and that he could wiggle his ears?) and watching the sun go down from the dunes. Another fond memory was laying upstairs and listening to the Doug firs sing in the wind and hearing the surf from beyond the Gray's Paintin' Place (that's what my dad called the house next door because owner Charles "Nony" Gray was a housepainter)."

Stephanie's father claimed that a sea captain had hanged himself in the abandoned carriage house on the property. "I have no clue where he would have heard that," she said. "Maybe in a bar. I remember feeling sad about it. Depending upon which bedroom I was sleeping in, I could see the carriage house from my window, and I do know that lights over there that were turned off at bedtime would be on in the morning and shades were up that had been down. Somehow, we never thought too much about that....I wasn't afraid. But I do think that's when I realized that maybe a person's spirit could stay attached to a place."

Like most Peninsula kids—both year-rounders and part-timers—Stephanie learned to drive on the beach. "I was only thirteen. I remember that my dad made me back the length of the Seaview Approach Road! It was sand and gravel back then—mostly sand—and was probably a good five hundred feet long."

At the time Crow Cottage was built, Ilwaco was just a small collection of wooden buildings—residences for its population of 150, plus a few retail establishments, a post office and several saloons. There was also a hotel and boardinghouse to accommodate the visitors who journeyed down the Columbia River in the summer to spend time away from the oppressive heat of Oregon's inland valleys. The town was nestled in the shelter of Baker's Bay—just a hop and a skip from the sandy beaches along the Pacific and possessing its own gently sloping bathing beach.

WHEALDONSBURG: A MATTER OF TIMING

Called *No'sk walakuthl* for centuries by the Chinook Indians, present-day Ilwaco had a somewhat muddled beginning from the time white settlers began to arrive. First came James Johnson, a former Hudson Bay Company bar pilot who moved his family to the site in 1849 and filed the first Donation Land Claim in the immediate area. Two years later, James D. Holman took a Donation Land Claim on Johnson's western border. In 1855, the Holmans moved to Portland, and that same year, their neighbors, the Johnsons, both died. Guardians for the Johnson children sold their claim to newly arrived Isaac Whealdon and family in 1858.

For several years, the Whealdons were the only white settlers in the area, and their homestead (which covered approximately the site of today's Ilwaco) was known to travelers as "Whealdonsburg." On November 26, 1860, the U.S. Postal Service established a post office at the Whealdons' home. The agency named it Pacific City Post Office in honor of the short-lived town (1850–52) on Cape Disappointment that had been vacated when the federal government appropriated the land to establish Fort Canby.

As far as is known, the area continued to be called Whealdonsburg until 1865, when the postal service again changed the name, this time to Unity to honor the increasing sentiment in the area concerning the War Between the States and to pay tribute to the growing numbers of soldiers at Fort Canby. Meanwhile, Holman continued to live in Portland but vacationed yearly on his land next to Whealdon.

Descendants of pioneers Mary Ann and Isaac Whealdon continue to live in the Ilwaco area and take an active interest in community affairs. *EFA.*

In 1873, Holman subdivided his Peninsula DLC, and at the county courthouse in Oysterville, he filed the plat for the town of Ilwaco. The name honored an Indian neighbor of the Holmans and Whealdons, Elowahka Jim, who was popular in the growing community. He was married to Elowahka, a daughter of one of Chinook chief Comcomly's wives, and was generally known by her name.

Whealdon, however, was not yet deterred in his desire to formalize his own town. In June 1892, he subdivided his land and filed a plan for the town of Whealdonsburg, but by then, the name Ilwaco had taken hold of the entire area. The Ilwaco city fathers did retain Whealdon's street names, which included references to his Quaker faith, local tree types and the first names of his wife, Mary Ann, and three daughters, Elizabeth, Eliza and Adelia.

THE FINNISH CONNECTION

The quiet getaway atmosphere would soon change, however. In 1879, B.A. Seaborg, a Finnish immigrant cannery worker in Astoria, moved to the north side of the river with his family to build the first cannery on Ilwaco's waterfront: the Aberdeen Packing Company. Immediately, the little town began to boom, and the prospects for Ilwaco's economic future brightened considerably.

Not only did Seaborg's cannery and fishing operation draw hopeful workers from the increasing immigrant population arriving in the Lower Columbia region, but numbers of Finnish bachelors also followed him from Astoria, seeking better work opportunities on the river and in the cannery. It wasn't long before Ilwaco began to take on a rough and rambunctious atmosphere.

By 1890, there were six saloons in town, and law-abiding citizens were loath to go out after dark, especially after work hours, when the saloons filled up, largely with unmarried men without "civilizing" ties to home and family. Bar fights and occasional shootings gave Ilwaco an unsavory reputation, and it wasn't until the gradual arrival of sweethearts and wives from "home" that the town atmosphere settled down. Meanwhile, prejudices grew. According to some sources, until the end of World War I, Finnish culture was dominant in Ilwaco. Finnish was the community language, and the ubiquitous sauna,* a familiar comfort from their home country, popped up in most Finnish backyards. Small-town life included lodges for the men, with auxiliary branches for the women, often with socialist overtones. As the twentieth century dawned, there were some Ilwaco residents who made little differentiation between "Finnish," "Socialist" and "Communist." Feelings often ran high, and vestiges of those early-day prejudices still linger.

"When we moved in," recalled Stephanie, "Viola Saari lived next door to our place in the house that had once belonged to her parents. She told me that her father had bached in our house when he first came to this country from Finland. I don't know if that meant he lived with a lot of other unmarried men or if he had the house all to himself until he got married.…Viola was in her eighties when we bought the house, and she died in 2000 at ninety-one. I wish I'd asked her more questions, but isn't that always the way?"

"Technically," said Stephanie, "the property is two lots. Two addresses, multiple utility bills, with Crow Cottage on one and, on the lot behind, a building that had been turned into a rental cottage by the time we entered the picture. Another old-timer neighbor, Edna Gray, told us that at one time it was a Finnish Bath House—apparently a large one."

Stephanie continued: "Actually, Edna said 'Communist Bath House,' but we knew what she meant. Edna said that it was added to the barn in the 1930s. Another clue to the building's use might be the once-upon-a-time carved graffiti in the entryway that someone, maybe Jon Kaino, said was carved by bathers/patrons who were waiting their turn in the sauna. In the years that we've owned the property, the graffiti has completely disappeared. I wish we'd thought to take a picture."

---

* Interestingly, *sauna* is the only Finnish word that has become a part of the English lexicon.

THE SAUNA

It was at the turn of the twentieth century that the greatest influx of immigrants arrived at the mouth of the Columbia. Among those who found the burgeoning salmon fishing industry both familiar and in need of workers were the Finns. They settled in Astoria on the Oregon side of the river and in Ilwaco on the Washington side. They brought with them their love of family, their strong work ethic and their cultural customs, including the sauna.

Although saunas have existed in other cultures, it is in Finland that they became entwined with every aspect of daily life. Traditionally, it was often the first structure a family built, and it would be used as a living and eating space, for matters of hygiene and, most importantly, for giving birth in an almost sterile environment. Saunas were basic to the Finnish way of life. And so it was in Ilwaco in the early twentieth century.

Traditional saunas are heated by wood, burned either in a stove with a chimney or by a stove with no chimney. The latter—a smoke-sauna (*savusauna*)—is the original sauna and believed by most Finns to be the best. The door is closed after the wood has burned down (and most of the smoke

"Grandpa Ziesmer's Sauna" was built eighty years ago, the first building on his property in the town of Naselle, just upriver from Ilwaco. *Stacy Katyryniuk.*

has escaped), leaving the embers to heat the sauna to the proper temperature, 80–110 °C (176–230 °F), but giving a soft heat and the aroma of wood smoke.

All saunas have a basket of rocks heated by the stove on which to throw water to increase the humidity. Called *löyly* in Finnish, the steam increases the feeling of heat and makes you sweat. Each sauna is considered to have its own character and its own distinctive *löyly*. The better the *löyly*, the more enjoyable the sauna.

While many Finnish homes had their own saunas, there were two privately run public saunas, and in addition, there was a community sauna called the Company Sauna in Ilwaco. In a reminiscence about growing up in Ilwaco in the 1890s, William Koski (1889–1974) wrote about "the large sauna bath where all the Finns on that side of Ilwaco would beat themselves with cedar switches in all that terrific heat till they looked like boiled lobsters. The sauna bath was the big thing on Saturdays, especially when the men had booze along. Then you could hear them raising Cain over most of the town. The sauna had certain rooms for entire families, and for women, and many a time we went for our bath when Ma would go into the steam room with a nursing baby in her arms, so I guess it must have been o.k. as it didn't hurt us any."

The Mystery Boiler

Stephanie and Dave said, "Judging by the fixtures and paneling in the bathroom, as well as kitchen cupboards, the sauna space was turned into a little cottage in the 1950s. There is a derelict barn attached to it, and though we'd like to take it down, we've been stymied by the very large boiler in the barn attic—probably more properly called the haymow or hayloft. The boiler is so big, it can't be readily removed."

Their assumption was that the boiler was used to heat water to meet the needs of a large family, or perhaps it was the hot water source for the communal sauna. "We soon learned, though, that although communal saunas were typical among the large Finn population here, it was the traditional dry heat saunas that were used—not wet heat like in Turkish baths."

And so, the precise purpose of that huge boiler remains a mystery. However, there are no shortage of ideas—mostly humorous—among the Finns of the area. "An interesting question!" one old-timer said. "Maybe they used it to heat the barn for the cows!" And then, on second thought: "Not likely, though—cows, themselves, seem to provide good heat for the barn! I could see someone using a large boiler for the *kiuas* [stove] and throwing water on it for steam, though."

Another man remembered, "A friend in Hibbing [Minnesota] used an old cast-iron heat register [the kind that stands up on the floor] in his sauna and drew steam from the city-wide, central steam system through the register for heat. That was one of the sweatiest saunas I've ever been in. The steam came from water thrown onto the heavy metal surface, no rocks, and I could see a heavy-duty boiler used in the same way. Those Finns were pretty resourceful!"

The grandson of an old logger had another idea. "Back in the days of the steam donkeys, the old water tanks were often repurposed in interesting ways. Maybe that boiler started out in the woods near here."

None of the explanations seemed adequate, and so the huge old boiler remains a mystery. When Dave climbed the stairs to the barn loft last summer, the mystery suddenly compounded. The boiler was gone! "Gone!" he exclaimed. "As in not there. All that remains is some ductwork." And he took a photograph to prove it.

Family visits to Crow Cottage have been frequent, even though the trip is not exactly a hop and a skip from Gig Harbor. Depending on which route is taken, the driving distance is either 149 or 175 miles, but presumably, the difference between the two only amounts to nine minutes. On paper. The drive can actually take as many as five hours depending on the Seattle/Tacoma/Olympia traffic, the weather, the route chosen and the time of day. But by now, the family are old hands at choosing among all the variables. Sometimes they actually make it in the three and a quarter hours the journey is "supposed" to require.

No matter how they have managed their trips over the years, the family has almost always made the trek in groups—perhaps family units, perhaps with friends, and usually with eager kids in tow. As the children (and now grandchildren) have reached their teen years, however, extracurricular activities often keep everyone busy in Gig Harbor. Stephanie and Dave are great kid supporters, so it was unusual that they would come to the beach if anything important was happening up north.

Then, four years ago, Stephanie's mom moved to the Tacoma Lutheran Retirement Center. Stephanie and Dave and family would soon move from

"I was absolutely gobsmacked when I learned that the old boiler was no longer up in the haymow," said Stephanie. *Dave Haeck.*

Gig Harbor to be nearby. Tacoma was closer to Ilwaco and the beach, but not by much. And it was becoming abundantly clear to Stephanie and Dave that if visits to the beach were to continue, they would sometimes have to make the trek alone. It was on the first such solitary visit that Stephanie heard the ghost.

FOOTSTEPS UPSTAIRS

"I don't think those footsteps upstairs really registered right away," said Stephanie, laughing. "I was down in the living room, reading, and though I was aware that someone else was in the house I didn't question it. There was *always* someone else in the house. That's the way we like it."

On this occasion, however, Stephanie had come to the beach on her own to ready the cottage for the next onslaught of guests and to have a little downtime from "life in the fast lane." As she heard more footsteps, she suddenly thought, "That's odd. I'm the only one here." There was

Whoever he is, he climbs the staircase only when there is just one person in the house. Never more than one. *Stephanie Frieze.*

nothing threatening or ominous feeling, so she just went on reading. "Eventually, it became silent, and I realized that whoever it was had gone away. I was sure it wasn't an intruder or any kind of threat, so it didn't occur to me to be afraid. I went upstairs to bed, as usual. End of story. Except I did tell Dave of my experience. He was skeptical."

Stephanie thinks it was two or three years later that, in his turn, Dave was alone at Crow Cottage. "He probably went down to mow or repair something. I don't remember. But when he came home, he said, "I finally heard your ghost." The situation had been similar. Dave was downstairs and heard a man walking around upstairs. "At least I thought it was a man. It didn't sound like a woman's footsteps," noted Dave.

Stephanie and Dave just assume that the man was a Finn—maybe Viola's father, maybe not. "I'm sure we came to that conclusion because of the mystery of the boiler and the stories of the Finnish Bath House," Stephanie said.

"We've heard him several times now. Maybe it's just that it's quieter in the house these days without all the young people. They're busy going to camp and trotting off to gymnastics and dancing competitions. We often have the house to ourselves. We actually listen for him these days."

"No matter who he is," said Dave and Stephanie, "we are delighted to have a ghost at Crow Cottage. Every old structure needs a ghost, don't you think? Especially a benign ghost like ours."

"Or is he?" Stephanie asked after a pause. "What do you think he's doing with that boiler?"

CHAPTER 6

THE BUILDING AT
1306 BAY AVENUE

In Ocean Park…

Madam X was shaking from the effort she was making.
We were shaking, too, but more from nerves.
—assistant to Madam X

The innocuous-looking structure toward the west end of Bay Avenue in Ocean Park has been there for years—as long as anyone now living can remember. And anyone who has known the area for any length of time is probably aware of the building's checkered past. It has served at least a dozen purposes, both commercial and residential, over the last century—reason enough for it to have a bit of a reputation. But not until very recently did anyone suspect that the building at number 1306 might be haunted!

The earliest remembered use of the building was as an ice cream parlor. What could be more innocent? Dorothy Trondsen Williams, who was born in Ocean Park in 1926, has a clear memory of going to Alice Burch's Ice Cream Parlor in her youth. What little girl wouldn't remember that? Strangely, though, she doesn't recall what kind of ice cream she looked forward to as a special treat. A cone? A dish? A favorite flavor? "Too long ago," she said.

I feel a lot like that myself when it comes to this particular building. Although I was born ten years after Dorothy, I do remember very clearly that in the fall of 1947, my grandfather Harry Espy asked me to ride with him in

For more than a century, the distinctive-looking house (*second from left*) at 1306 Bay Avenue has served many purposes, both commercial and residential. *SPP.*

his old Plymouth and witness the mailing of a very important document. I have no idea what it was or why it couldn't be mailed from Oysterville, but I do remember sitting in the car and watching Papa walk across the street and drop the parcel in the big post office box in front of the Ocean Park Post Office. And I remember that it was dark out but that the attractive little white building was clearly visible in the light from the car's bright headlamps.

In retrospect, I believe that he was mailing tax documents and that he was worried about remembering. Indeed, within the next five or six years, Papa's fine mind fogged up entirely with dementia—"premature senile decay" they called it then. But during the 1947–48 school year—the year I lived in Oysterville and went to school in Ocean Park—he was still driving, helping me with my math homework and telling the best stories ever.

REMEMBERING IT DIFFERENTLY

Our neighbor Les Driscoll has a different memory of the building during that same period, the mid-'40s. As it happens, Les was in my seventh-grade class, and he remembered that his family lived in that very structure from 1946 to 1960. "My folks bought it from Roy Harris," he recalled. "He had a body and fender shop about five blocks south of the Ocean Park Grade School." The building had been vacant for a long time when the Driscolls bought it. "It was an old building and needed a lot of work," Les said. "There was no running water. My dad put in the plumbing and built a garage."

So, my memory of the building being a post office in 1947 was totally wrong! Hard to believe. I felt as though the structure itself was playing tricks with me. However, just about the time I learned of the Driscolls' tenure there, I ran across a photograph among some family keepsakes. It showed the distinctive little structure clearly with an "Ocean Park Post Office" sign prominently displayed on its east wall. There were a number of people—adults and children—in front of the building, on the porch and on the bench to the west. They looked to be dressed in clothing and hats typical of the early twentieth century—way before my 1947 memory.

She had asked two of us to assist her this time. When she had done her usual "drive-by" the day before, she felt a lot of negative energy surging out from the house. A lot! There were three people there—a boy, a woman and a really big, really, really mean guy. She knew she'd need help. More help than usual.

—assistant to Madam X

This early twentieth-century photograph shows the building in use as a U.S. Post Office, just as "remembered" by the author some years later. *EFA.*

We approached the building in the usual way. We first put a little black salt across the doorstep to give the house an extra barrier against evil. Then we said the Lord's Prayer and lit the candle, asking that the white light of protection surround us. Madam X motioned for the two of us to walk close beside her as we entered.

—assistant to Madam X

I've still not settled the "Post Office Question" in my mind. Obviously, what I remember is wrong, even though it is perfectly clear to me. But why do I remember *that* building on *that* side of Bay Avenue in Ocean Park? And why does my memory say "post office"? Why was my memory thirty or forty years out of sync with reality? Bothersome to ponder. Haunting, really.

One more mention, at least by implication, of a post office in that location can be found in *Postmarked Washington: Pacific and Wahkiakum Counties* by Guy Reed Ramsey: "Mrs. Emma P. Campbell [the third postmaster since the Ocean Park Post Office was established on June 28, 1906] operated the post office in a vacated store building on Bay Street." That was from 1919 until 1927, when, according to Ramsey, "William C. Pearson erected a post office building on the north side of the same street." The one on the north side of Bay is the one that all the other old-timers agree on.

No one seems to remember much about the building during the 1970s and '80s. By the 1990s, though, a goldsmith had bought the building to serve as his studio and retail shop. "Anthony Garzino, Master Goldsmith" read the sign over the porch. It seemed pretty uptown for Ocean Park to have a goldsmith right on the main drag, but no sooner was the word out than folks from all over the Peninsula were at his door.

ENTER: CATE GABLE

Somewhere along the line—after the goldsmith but before the landscaper—the building was purchased by Cate Gable, well-known local writer and musician. There was a series of renters there in the twenty or so years Cate owned the building. All of them loved it. None of them stayed long. The building seemed endlessly adaptable, whether used as a residence—Cate had a shower added to the bathroom to complete the residential amenities—or as a business, or as both.

When Cate bought the building from Tony in 2004, Joy Weber already had her Farmers Insurance business there. Joy continued to rent from

"The Fairy Store," as people called it, was magical and mysterious and just a wee bit menacing all at the same time. *Author's collection.*

Cate, and when she retired in 2008, Leslie Ferguson took over the business. Since then, it has housed Ed Strange's landscaping business and the first rendition of the Bay Avenue Gallery, with Bette Lu Krause and Sue Raymond as founders.

My own "Kuzzin Kris" Jones, the opera singer, lived and worked there for more than a year. Immediately after that, the building housed "Fairy People" Mike and Debbie Schramer, with their phantasmagorical shop and its thousands of whimsical objects—from little dolls and figurines to inventive musical instruments and fairy castles and oh so much more!

Kuzzin Kris had her baby grand piano in the large front room, where she gave voice lessons. There was plenty of space left over for her meditation group, or if she was entertaining, she could easily seat and serve eight at her dining room table in that same spacious room. Only the kitchen was small—a galley-style arrangement that we referred to as "a one-butt kitchen"—depending, perhaps, on the size of the occupants' derrieres!

We had hardly stepped beyond the doorway when the boy and the woman met us. They were very frightened. They told Madam X that the mean guy wouldn't let them leave. "You can go whenever you want," she told them. "You don't have to stay." And that's all it took. They were gone!

—assistant to Madam X

When the Fairy People took over, the space seemed to increase and diminish threefold, all at the same time! There were enough whimsical curiosities, one within another and within still another, that space and time seemed endless. And yet, with very little room to walk or move around between exhibits, the space closed in around the visitor—it was magical but in a strange and slightly unnerving way.

Perhaps it was only a coincidence that the building's troubles began shortly after the Fairy People moved out. Cate was pleased that she had rented the house to a couple new to the Peninsula—a teacher and her handyman husband. They, too, were well satisfied. It seemed perfect for them. But then in May, just as the school year was winding down, Cate got a call. "Our toilet won't flush." The troubles had begun.

"Wouldn't you know I was a thousand miles away in the desert in Arizona at my annual poetry retreat?" Cate sighed. "I worked with the plumber long distance. We had the septic tank cleaned out… but that didn't solve the problem. Leonard Taylor designed a new system, but before the installation could be completed, I was told that all the pipes in the house would need to be lowered by four inches."

I lit the sage, but it and the candle kept going out. Madam X relit them again and again and sprayed the holy water to the left and right and in front of us as we slowly made our way through the living room. "Get closer to me," she kept telling us and the three of us held hands.

—assistant to Madam X

No Crawl Space

"I called another plumber—someone I'd worked with before, and he went over to take a look."

"I can't lower the pipes until you get it excavated. There isn't enough crawl space."

Soon, however, the problem seemed well on its way to being solved. The plumber's son-in-law would be happy to get under there and do a little excavating. A few days and a lot of dollars later, the excavating was completed. But the old post-and-pier foundation—always solid and reliable—had been seriously damaged in the process.

Cate called a halt to all of the repairs and began the search for some foundation professionals to bid the job. No luck locally, so she went across the river, which, of course, means out of state and into Oregon, which often causes other ramifications. Finally, she managed to get a doable bid but no guarantees on a timeline. It was now September. "Maybe we could get started in December," she was told.

"By now I was feeling that something was going on beyond the usual old house renovation woes. But I couldn't see a way forward except to

"The new septic system was only the beginning. It never occurred to me that the building might be haunted!" Cate said later. *Cate Gable.*

keep on moving ahead. So, I called my friend Phil Allen. He's a retired architect from California with roots right there on Bay Avenue. I trusted his judgement, and when he suggested that he could draw up a plan, I began to be hopeful again. Under the house he went, accompanied by Shane the Garden Guy— Phil's wife's garden helper whom she reluctantly shared for the duration of the job."

There was a long pause in Cate's narrative. And then…a deep breath. "But that's just the Repair Track," she said. Say what? She and I were having this discussion almost a year after the fact—a year during which Cate had said very little about the problems. "It was just too traumatic," she said. "But, yes. There was also a Sales Track. It paralleled the Repair Track! I think I need to make a couple of timelines. With overlays!" she laughed.

Madam X gripped our hands ever more tightly. Once again, she repeated the blessing—the Lord's Prayer. "This is a very angry, very strong person—stronger than I can handle by myself!" Madam X told us. "Stay close," she said again.

—assistant to Madam X

DEEP ROOTS IN OCEAN PARK

Although Phil Allen grew up in California, his Peninsula roots are deep. As he worked on the house at 1306 Bay Avenue, he could look across the street and a block east at the Taylor Hotel, built in 1887 by his great-great-grandparents Adelaide and Bill Taylor. The romantic story of their daughter Maud's marriage to shipwrecked Scotsman William Begg is one of the oft-told tales on stormy Peninsula nights.

Phil was a summer kid on the Long Beach Peninsula. His memories of those summers of the 1950s and '60s are what drew him back to retire a decade or so ago. His eyes light up as he tells of childhood treks out to the beach with Great-Grandpa Willie to the place where the superstructure of the *Glenmorag* was still visible.

"He'd go so many paces north and say, 'Dig here' and I'd dig and...there would be the bow! Then we'd pace so many steps in the opposite direction. 'Dig here' he'd say. And there would be the stern! Now that was really, truly digging for treasure!" Years later, Phil would go to Glasgow to see the *Glenlee*, the restored sister ship of the *Glenmorag*, and he never stops hoping that the wreck he and his great-grandfather dug for will appear again out in front of Ocean Park.

It was Willie Begg who taught Phil how to dig clams and how to fish in Loomis Lake. "They used to stock it with trout in those days," he remembered. "And then there were the salmon over in the river!" Phil was seventeen when Great-Grandpa Willie died in 1964 at the very respectable age of eighty-nine. And by then, Phil had discovered girls! "There were so many girls here at the beach,"

William Begg with the *Glenmorag*'s figurehead. As "yard art," it remained on display for years at the Begg home in Ocean Park. *Allen Family Collection.*

he remembered. "It wasn't like that at home in California! But more importantly, there were lakes and streams and rivers for fishing, woods calling to be explored and a beach full of treasures to find. I knew that someday I'd live here year-round."

Phil and his wife live in Long Beach. On any early morning, you might find him fishing at Black Lake in Ilwaco or setting off to explore Cape Disappointment...or, not so long ago, on his belly under a friend's house, lending his expertise to a puzzling problem.

An Offer to Buy

Along about the time the Fairy People were thinking of leaving Ocean Park, Cate arrived home late one afternoon to find a letter waiting for her. It was from a woman who said that she'd like to buy the house on Bay Avenue. "Really? Buy it?" Cate said. "I didn't know who she was, but I called her that very night; we had coffee at Adelaide's and agreed on a price. It was an unbelievable stroke of luck."

The potential buyer was working with a realtor across the river in Astoria, and that began the trouble on the Sales Track. Number 1306 Bay Avenue, Ocean Park, is, of course, in Washington. Granted, only twenty-nine miles and the Columbia River separate it from Astoria, Oregon. And granted, too, many people live on one side of the river and work on the other. There are even commercial enterprises, including banks, that do business in Washington and Oregon. However, 1306 Bay Avenue would not be so lucky. My hopeful buyer was doing business with an Oregon institution and was told that she'd have to transfer everything—all her paperwork, all the time she'd already put into the transaction—to their Seattle branch.

"I don't think a single one of my feathers ruffled at the news," Cate said. "During the past year, my expectations for anything going smoothly had long since vanished. In fact, slowly surfacing was the niggling little thought that something very out of the ordinary was at work here. Finally, the persistent buyer got the paper work together, we met with a realtor and...well, I just couldn't quite bring myself to sign. Not yet. I'm not sure why. It just didn't feel right."

The work on the plumbing was finally progressing apace, and things were looking more positive. Cate and the buyer kept in touch, and finally it was

Cate who called a local realtor and had papers drawn up. But it was another false start! "Just as I was ready to exhale, the Title Company called," Cate remembered.

"You don't own the building," they said. "Well, you don't own all the building."

"What?! For nearly twenty years I'd been maintaining it, making repairs, paying property taxes on it and now…I DON'T OWN IT???"

It seemed that Tony had never done the final title transfer. They needed to sign additional papers to release a small lien that they had all agreed to while Cate was finalizing the sale of her home in California. The lien had been paid off, but the final paperwork had never been signed and filed with the title company.

Cate began searching for Tony and his wife, Liz. "The first thing I learned was that when they left this area, they had gone to Mexico. But where? Before any answers to that question were forthcoming, I also heard that Tony had died. But the building had been in both their names. Now what? Was Liz his sole heir? How could I get in touch with her? Was her name still Garzino? Who remembered her and where was she? How to find out?"

Not only was that guy's energy strong, but Madam X was getting old and her own strength was waning. We didn't know it then, but Cate was the last person she would help with a house problem.

—assistant to Madam X

WHEN IN DOUBT

Cate went directly to her friends on Facebook. "And wonder of wonders! My friend Rita Nicely had Liz's e-mail address and phone number. Under the circumstances, I thought it best to phone her and, of course, began my conversation with condolences for her loss. With that, things went downhill and uphill simultaneously!"

"What!? Tony's not dead!" Liz said in amazement. "He's right here! Here, let me hand the phone to him and you can talk to him yourself!"

And so, Tony and Liz signed the required title transfer, the building was finally Cate's and she thought that a happy outcome was in sight. She and a painter friend went over to do a little touch-up painting around a window that had been replaced in the back bedroom. That's when they saw the little, inch-long crack in the new glass pane. The painter thought he could repair this small blemish, but when he placed the window-repair kit to the glass…*zzzzap!* Like lightning, the crack extended upward for twelve inches and soon raced to fill the entire new window.

"That did it. There was no longer a doubt in my mind that something very peculiar was going on with this building. I remembered a discussion I'd had a few years back with a friend who told me that she'd met a woman who was a—for lack of a better term—ghostbuster. I wasted no time in making arrangements for her to see what she could do to help." The problem was that the real estate appraiser was supposed to arrive in mere days.

Madam X drove by the little building that very day and immediately learned that it housed more than one presence. "That afternoon," Cate said, "Madam X reported that there was a young boy, a woman and a really big, really, really mean guy in residence and that she would certainly need more help for this job." It would require herself and not one but two experienced helpers to rid Cate's house at 1306 of its ghostly and mysterious problems. "Take as many people as you need!" Cate told her.

"We just need to make our plan and get some supplies," Madam X said. "We'll go tomorrow night."

"I was a little concerned about that," Cate remembered. "I wasn't sure what they would be doing in there, but I thought the 'supplies' sounded ominous. I wanted them to do whatever they needed to do to get rid of the problems, but the appraiser and the new owner were coming the next morning and I didn't want to freak them out. I don't think there's a law here in Washington that you have to disclose ghost activity," she told me. "But still."

"I went over very early the next the morning with a couple of friends," Cate continued. "Everything looked neat and tidy except for a little black salt on the window sills. And you'll never believe the appraisal! It was for $5,000 more than our agreed-to selling price. The buyer had equity in the house from the get-go!"

Cate called Madam X, who told her that all was well. "The young boy and the woman left right away," she said. "In fact, they were just waiting for someone to give them permission and to help them escape! But the third presence—the really big, really, really mean guy—was another story. He was difficult. But he's gone now."

As we got near that broken window in the back, Madam X called for the Archangel Gabriel to help us. She told him, "We need your strength!" That was a first for me. I'd never known her to call on her spirit guide before. By now she was perspiring with the effort. So were we… but probably more from fear.

—assistant to Madam X

Finally, the really big, really, really mean guy left through that rear window—the same way he had entered in the first place. But before he left, he said his name was Jacob Jacobsen. Later, we found three very large footprints in the sandy soil outside the house.

—assistant to Madam X

"And that was the end of it," Cate said. "As far as I can learn, Jacob Jacobsen is not a name that means anything to anyone in Ocean Park—not to the old-timers and not to those who live and work in the area now. Not that we know of, anyway," she added. "I hope we don't hear of him again!"

Recent changes to the exterior of the little house have made it almost unrecognizable to those who have known it over the years. Should the really big, really, really mean guy be looking to reenter his old haunt, perhaps it will be equally unidentifiable to him. "We can only hope," said Cate.

CHAPTER 7

THE GIRL IN THE WALL

In Chinook…

Hanna! Hanna!" she called. "Hanna! Wake up! Wake up Now!"
"It was Grandma Provo. She always called me Hanna. And never mind that she'd already been in her grave a year or more. Even when she was living, I knew she had the third eye. We had a special relationship, and I know she'll always look after me."

Johanna and David Gustafson and their eighteen-month-old daughter, Milly, had moved into the house on Evelyn Road in Chinook in the early autumn that year. "It was our second night in the house," she said. "I woke up to see the entire backyard on fire. The two barns behind the house were in flames. And it was hot! So, so hot!'

"I grabbed Milly and called 911. David was out the door and hooking up the garden hose to stop the flames that were already attacking the back wall of the house. I don't know if I'm remembering it in a blur or in a smoky haze or in slow-motion," she said. "The Chinook Fire Department was there in no time! They were amazing. But even so, both barns burned to the ground."

When all was said and done, the firemen were able to save the house. Only the rear wall needed replacing. "David was an absolute hero," Johanna remembered. "When it was over, he still had the hose in his hand—about eighteen inches of it, including the nozzle. The rest had melted to uselessness!"

THE THIRD EYE

The third eye, sometimes called "the mind's eye" or "inner eye," is a mystical concept concerning a speculative invisible eye. It is usually depicted as located on the forehead and is thought to provide perception beyond ordinary sight. Often associated with the third eye are religious visions, clairvoyance, the ability to observe chakras and auras, precognition and out-of-body experiences. Those who are said to have the capacity to utilize their third eyes are sometimes known as *seers*.

When asked about her association with the concept of the third eye, Johanna said, "I'm not sure. I've just always known Grandma Provo had it. She'd know things ahead of when they actually happened. After she, herself, passed, people told me that she had shared ahead of time with them that their own loved ones were going to die."

Having hunches, knowing good news or bad news before it happens, having strong intuition—these are all things that were just "part of Grandma Provo," according to Johanna. "I've never questioned the truth of what she says—even now and even if it comes to me in my sleep!"

THE RENOVATING BEGINS

Johanna and David had been planning to do some renovations to the old house anyway. "The fire just sped up our timeline a bit. The Wilson Brothers of Chinook began on that back wall almost immediately. Gradually, over the next few years, we completely redid the bathroom. We tore out all the carpeting and took the floors right down to the original fir planks. We kept the good parts—the wainscoting and the bones of the old icebox in the kitchen. I use it as a pantry now."

The two-story farmhouse was built in 1902, and although no one now knows for sure, it seems likely that Daniel Williams built the house for his bride, Florence Goulter Williams. It was the year they were married and right at the peak of Chinook's glory years. Their marriage marked the union of two of the leading pioneer families of Pacific County and was blessed with two children—their son, Berwyn, born in 1902, and their daughter, Catherine, born a few years later.

Above: This picture of the Daniel Williams House, shown before the porch was enclosed, was probably taken in the mid-1930s. *Sharron Goulter Mattson Collection.*

Left: Daniel and Florence Goulter Williams, with children Berwyn and Catherine, circa 1916. *Sharron Goulter Mattson Collection.*

CHINOOK: THE GLORY YEARS

"Chinook is a town of attractive homes, clean streets, large yards, and comfortable surroundings, with little of the friction encountered in the outside world," the *Chinook Observer* was pleased to report in 1910. "Life here is simple, peaceful and natural. The people are charitable, sociable and helpful. The severities of existence do not appear in Chinook. Land is cheap, food is abundant on land and in water, and the 'wolf' of poverty is a thing unknown."

Chinook had been settled in the late nineteenth century by fishermen, about half of whom were from Scandinavia or other maritime countries. The town's entire population of seven hundred was supported by salmon fishing, and by 1915, when the Chinook Packing Company was established, many of the salmon supplied to the cannery came from traps placed along the northern bank of the Columbia River. As many as ten thousand pounds of salmon were processed through the cannery in a single day when the fish were running.

Dan Williams Grocery. *From left to right*: Rab Hall, Howard Williams and Dan Williams. *Sharron Goulter Mattson Collection.*

According to *Polk's Directory*, the flourishing town on Baker Bay sustained a weekly newspaper, the *Observer*, and supported two churches, Methodist and Evangelical Lutheran; a public school with an average attendance of 120 pupils; a fine, two-story public hall; eight business houses; two hotel buildings; three lodges of Redmen and Maccabees; a post office; and a salmon hatchery. It also had long-distance telephone service, a daily (except Sunday) stage from Ilwaco six miles west and a tri-weekly steamer to Astoria and other points along the Columbia River. Daniel Williams owned the grocery store and dealt in "fancy groceries, flour, and feed."

Recreational activities included hunting and fishing, intermural baseball games, church activities, saloon goings-on, a twelve-member brass band, the Chinook Debating Society and entertainments at Chinook Hall, including orations, political meetings and moving picture shows. As the twentieth century got underway in Chinook, Washington, the town seemed to have something for everybody.

"Even though the house was more than a hundred years old when we bought it, we were only the third family to own it—but the fourth family to live in it," said Johanna. "I think about that a lot when I'm trying to figure out who the ghosts are that we live with. It stands to reason—at least to me—that they were associated with the house in some way."

Johanna and David bought the house from Dan and Lynn Whealdon. "They were only the second, or maybe the third family to own it," Johanna said, smiling. "It depends upon how you look at it. They bought it in the early 1990s from Dan's grandparents, Dan and Evelyn Coyle Whealdon, and *they* had bought it from the Williams in 1944. So, there were two family groups from one family that lived in the house— the grandparents for about fifty years and then the grandson and his family for another ten years. I might not have the dates quite right, but you get the idea." Then she was back to her main concern: the ghosts in the house.

"One more thing, though," she noted. "This is the only house on Evelyn Road here in Chinook. I imagine the street went in sometime after World War II—about the time the elder Whealdons moved in. Maybe they had a say in what to name the street and called it 'Evelyn' after Mrs. Whealdon. But isn't it interesting that two generations later their grandson would marry Lynn whose real name is Evelyn?" She looked so pleased with the thought that I couldn't help but agree with her! Interesting, indeed.

The Man in the Pantry

"It wasn't very long after we'd finished cleaning up the fire mess that Milly had a really scary encounter. Scary to me, that is," Johanna said. "I don't think Milly was old enough to quite grasp it." Johanna had arranged a shelf in the newly renovated pantry—a shelf of treats for Milly. On it was a selection of appropriate snacks from which she could choose for herself, but only after Mom or Dad had given their okay.

"Milly and I were working in the living room, and she asked if she could get a snack. She was back in a few minutes and told me there was a man in the pantry. He wanted her to go with him."

Even now, almost fourteen years later, Johanna's voice rises as she tells the story. "I absolutely freaked. I was outta that room and into the kitchen in a nanosecond. But…nothing. Nobody. And no evidence of anyone. All I could think of was those stories of the gypsies who used to come to Chinook in the olden days—a hundred years ago or so. All the kids around here grew up knowing about the gypsies, and if they saw anyone suspicious, they were to run home. Right now!"

The pantry incident was never explained, and Johanna and David forgot about it. Mostly. Meanwhile, during the week, when David was working and the weather was nice, Johanna and Milly began working outside in the backyard. Milly would take turns "helping" and then playing, and gradually the garden began to take shape. "Sometimes I'd feel like someone was watching us, and two or three times we saw an old lady looking out of Milly's bedroom window at us. She was sort of behind the curtains, but she seemed to be smiling. She seemed nice, and I'm sure I smiled back," Johanna remembered.

She didn't think much about it at the time, nor did Milly ever comment. It wasn't until the girl fell out of the wall that she and David began to wonder what was going on.

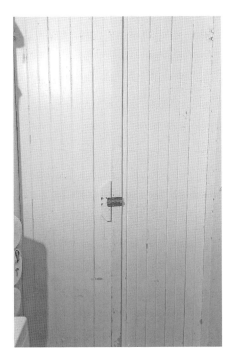

This page: The old-fashioned cooler has been transformed into a modern "pantry" where family snacks are kept and where, apparently, mysterious men hang out. *Johanna Gustafson.*

"No. It wasn't a real girl. It was a photograph. A very old, very fragile photograph. I was working on the staircase wall. The wallpaper had been applied right over the exterior siding, and when I pulled at the wooden door frame, something just floated down from above my head. It just sort of came waffling down—a picture of a lovely little girl—but there was nothing written on the back. No identification at all. I don't know why, but I got it in my head that it had something to do with a child who had died. And right afterward, down came a brown, wooden checker. *Thunk!*"

ASKING FOR HELP

"I was really curious about that picture. The little girl—about three, I'd say—had blond hair and was dressed in an old-fashioned-looking dress. There was a big dog with her," Johanna said, wistfully. "I showed it to

If the Gypsies Come into Town...

Most people who grew up anywhere on the Peninsula in the 1930s and '40s can remember the whispers about gypsies and the admonition, especially in summer, not to talk to strangers and to run right home if the gypsies came into town. I can't remember if we even knew what gypsies looked like, but the stories of kids getting snatched and carried away rated right up there with ghost stories. As far as I know, none of us ever met a gypsy (properly called "Romani") face to face. Not those of us who lived on the Peninsula proper, that is.

For Chinook residents, it might have been different. Newspaperman Dale L. Plumb was born in Chinook in 1922 and spent his early childhood there. He wrote about the "real gypsies" who had a camp at the south end of town each summer. "The warnings not to go near the camp or they would carry me away still seem valid," he wrote in the summer 1992 issue of *Sou'wester* magazine.

The camp Plumb referred to may have been located near "where Chinook County Park is now"—just before the entrance to Fort Columbia. Other people, including my cousin Kris, remember stories of the camp being in the opposite direction, "where the airport is now," to the north between Chinook and Ilwaco. The "airport," simply an asphalt runway 2,080 by 50 feet with few other amenities, was constructed in 1937.

Whether or not the Romani come to the Peninsula these days, they still have a large presence in the Pacific Northwest. They began arriving in Oregon in 1864 with Kalderash families, a Romani subgroup, settling in the area between 1880 and 1920. Today, Oregon's Romani population is the largest in the United States, with Portland being the epicenter.

my friend Sharron Mattson. She's a Goulter, and I thought maybe she might recognize the girl if she was Dan and Florence Goulter Williams's daughter, but she didn't. And besides, Sharron knew that daughter very well. She was quite a bit older than Sharron, and she and her brother called her 'Aunt Cat', though I don't think she was really their aunt."

At Sharron's suggestion, Johanna took the photograph over to the Columbia Pacific Heritage Museum and showed it to Ellen Wallace. "Ellen has worked there forever, and she's probably looked at a gazillion pictures. She couldn't help me with the girl, but she thought the dog looked kind of familiar. We gave it some time—you know, to percolate—but it never came clear to her. I think she's still keeping her eye out if she's working in the photo archives."

So, Johanna carefully placed the checker and the photo in her old jewelry box, and she and David continued with their house projects. By 2007, they were ready to begin with the bathroom remodel. Their good friends Michele and Dave Marshman had done a lot of remodeling on their own place in Chinook, and they readily agreed to help.

"The first time we cut into the wall," Dave remembered, "we heard a man groaning—or that's what it sounded like."

"And," continued Johanna, "we all heard a man's footsteps upstairs. He was walking up above us and walked right through a wall that we knew was there. Dave was on a ladder and some insulation was thrown at him, and then a man made a sound like he was clearing his throat. We were all a bit freaked."

"Then, later," Michele remembered, "Dave was alone in the house when he heard boots walking right overhead. He ran out of the house and waited for someone to be there with him. He didn't want to be there alone again," she laughed. "About that time, Johanna and family were going to be out of town. We took advantage of the house being empty and placed a digital recorder there overnight. But an hour later, it was turned off and moved slightly from where we had placed it….One more creepy thing: the light in the laundry—one of those kinds hanging on a cord from the ceiling—started swinging in small circles for no reason. Definitely weird."

That was when they decided to do a cleansing of the whole house. "Dave and I had done a couple of other smudgings, and so we knew a little bit about it," Michele went on, "so the four of us talked it over and decided it sure couldn't hurt."

Things were quiet in the house for a few years. "Every once in a while, I'd think about all those things that had happened. It was clear to me the house was, or at least had been haunted, and I decided to ask the Lutheran minister if he would come and give the house a blessing. Just for good measure," said Johanna. "Just for reassurance." But when Johanna tried to call the minister, she found that he was out of town for a few months. So, she let the matter rest.

When shown this picture of Catherine Williams with her great-grandmother Jenny Goulter, Johanna thought she might be the girl in the wall. *Sharron Goulter Mattson Collection.*

Milly's little brother, Oscar, was born the last day of 2008, and a few days later, "just after New Year's in 2009, I finally had the pastor come to bless the house. I felt better about things then, and until a year or so ago, I thought everything was alright," she remembered.

"But then I was talking to the kids about some of it—not the really scary parts, just some of the weird, unexplained stuff, and Oscar said that something strange had happened to him too! He said it was a few years back, when he was three or four: a big hairy dog came into the living room to play with him. Just that once. He said he hoped for a long time that the dog would come back, but it never did."

Johanna went to her jewelry box to find the picture of the little girl with the big hairy dog to see if Oscar could identify it, but it was gone. So was the brown checker. "I looked everywhere," she told me. "So maybe we aren't through with all of this yet."

CHAPTER 8

PROBLEMS IN THE NEIGHBORHOOD

In Klipsan Beach…

If you keep your eyes peeled as you head north out of "downtown" Klipsan Beach, an unnamed road leads west into the trees. A large sign says, "Private Road/Dead End," but somehow, the narrow tree-lined drive looks too inviting to pass up. The five houses at its end are nestled in the lee of the primary dune, and although it can't be seen from the road, the visitor just *knows* there must be a path down to the beach behind at least one of the houses.

The properties are well kept, and the homes, though moderately sized, appear substantial. Not beach cabins. More like year-round homes built, perhaps, a few decades ago. They don't "match" one another. Each seems to have its own character and age. Each has weathered well but differently from the others—as though they arrived separately and at different times and are still keeping a bit of distance from one another. Not physical distance exactly. Something else.

The owner of the middle house approached Madam X a few years ago. Her work, she said, kept her in the city from time to time, and lately she'd had an uneasy feeling whenever she came back to the Peninsula after an absence. Nothing specific. Just a bad feeling. A very bad feeling. She was beginning to think about selling.

Blond, blue-eyed Helen is, perhaps, middle-aged—old enough to have a daughter just graduating from college. She's been coming to the Peninsula all her life, and she has seen to it that "the beach" (as many locals refer to the Long Beach Peninsula) has become a part of life for her family as well. "My husband and I finally bought a house here when our daughter was about ten. We couldn't leave our jobs in the city, but we were here at the beach as often as we could be."

For a few years, they advertised the house as a "vacation rental" to help defray the expense of a second home. "People always said they loved it," Helen said. "But sometimes they wrote strange things in the House Book. And very few of them ever rented from us again. It was odd. And our neighbors, especially the one to the north, began to be more and more… difficult."

MORE TO THE STORY

Madam X drove by the house to get a feel for things. "I'm not sure I was even home that day," Helen said. "She called in the evening and said that we definitely had some problems. We arranged that she would come over the very next day. I was watching out for her, and when she drove up, she stopped in front of the house, grabbed her witching stick out of the trunk and headed right around the house and out into the dunes. Just like she'd been here a million times before! Two women followed her, and I fell into line behind them."

The four women walked single file on the well-used, sandy path toward the beach. "Madam X led the way. We had hardly gotten down the steps before my neighbor (the one to the north) was out on her deck, yelling at us!"

"'What are you doing out there,' she wanted to know! Not that it was any of her business. We were on our own property, not hers! But as quick as a wink, one of the helpers called back to her. 'We're looking for a ring,' she said. 'Helen thinks she dropped it out here.' That was brilliant! She had no retort, and in fact, she went back inside. But I have no doubt that she was watching though her big picture window."

Meanwhile, Madam X didn't break stride—not for a second. As she walked, she swung the witching stick back and forth, back and forth. Before too many steps, it began bouncing up and down, "kind of frantically," Helen said. "It was indicating an area on the north side of the path. Madam X told us to dig! 'Just scrape some of that dry sand away,' she told us. And then she just stood there, very quiet."

Like many homes on the Peninsula's western side, Helen's place has a well-used path through the dunes to the beach. *Vicki Carter.*

Helen described hearing a one-sided conversation. "Why are you here?" Madam X asked. And then, "Do you want to leave?"

"Of course, we could only hear and see Madam X. But it was obvious that she was actually talking to someone and actually hearing a response. Then she turned to me and asked if I wanted these people to leave. I didn't really care, as long as they weren't causing trouble. Madam X told them that. And she talked to them almost as you would talk to young children, telling them they could stay but they had to behave and not bother people in the houses or on the paths," Helen said.

Apparently, they were part of a local Indian tribe from very long ago. Something had happened to all of them at once. Madam X couldn't tell if they had drowned or if they had become ill or what. "It seems odd to tell about it," Helen said, "but at the time it all seemed very logical. We all know that the Chinooks have lived here on the Peninsula since early times—way before whites came here. Early explorers 'gifted' them with smallpox and other diseases—almost wiped them out."

SINCE THE BEGINNING

According to the legends of the Chinookan people of the Shoalwater Bay region, they have been living in the area that is now Pacific County, Washington, "since the beginning." Archaeologists seem to concur, saying that 12,000 BPE (Before Present Era) is the earliest date of human presence in the Pacific Northwest and that prior to outside contact, tens of thousands of First Peoples were living in Chinook lands.

They lived in more than forty Chinook settlements located at the mouths of the Nemah, Naselle, Willapa and Bone Rivers, as well as at Nahcotta, Oysterville, Goose Point, Bruceport, Tokeland and Grayland. Villages of plank houses in these locations were populated during the winter months. Their inland locations offered protection from the severe coastal weather, and their proximity to Willapa Bay ensured access to plentiful shellfish and fishing sites along the streams and rivers that flowed into it.

At winter's end, the plank houses were dismantled, leaving only the framework, and families moved to their summer fishing grounds along the Columbia River, utilizing the same planks to set up their homes there. Spring and summer were a time of great abundance. After the First Salmon Ceremony, the Chinook salmon continued to run for several weeks, followed by another run that began in late July. Other salmon runs followed, and it

"Shores of Shoalwater Bay" is the title the photographer gave for this view of Chinook Indians in their cedar canoes circa 1913. *Edward S. Curtis.*

wasn't until the days grew short and the rain fell with regularity that the people returned to their protected villages, away from the river winds.

At both summer and winter villages and at multiple seasonal camps, every imaginable fish, mammal and plant was harvested—both for subsistence and for cultural purposes, not the least of which involved the exchange of goods up and down the coast, as well as along the Columbia and into the interior of the Northwest. When the first Euro-Americans made contact with the peoples of the Lower Columbia region in the mid-sixteenth century, they found them to be canny, sophisticated traders and able-bodied seamen. Their cedar canoes, wrought from a single tree, were often huge and especially designed for rough waters. Canoe travel not only linked their villages along the rivers, bays and sea but also allowed the Chinook people trade opportunities far to the north, south and east of their traditional lands.

Unfortunately, however, none of their sophisticated skills could prevent the onslaught of diseases to which they had no immunity. Although there is no proof, there has been speculation that the West Coast participated in the first great pandemic of introduced epidemic disease—smallpox in 1519 and the years following—which had been introduced to the mainland concurrent with Cortez's conquest of Mexico. The earliest documented smallpox epidemic in Oregon was in 1781. In subsequent years, other devastating epidemics of smallpox, malaria, fever/ague and measles also took their toll. Conservative estimates put the Lower Columbian Chinook population at fifteen thousand before white contact. By 1835, nine-tenths of the population had been "swept away," according to Dr. John McLoughlin, chief factor of the Hudson Bay Company at Fort Vancouver (1824–46).

No sooner had things settled down on the path than Madam X led the group back up to the house. "We have a half basement with windows all along the west side," Helen said. "When we crested the dune and could see the house, Madam X pointed to the northwest corner and asked, 'What's behind those windows?' I told her it was a small room—almost an alcove."

"What's in it?" she asked. "What's in that room?"

A TROUBLING DESK

This drawing approximates the decorative lion's head carving that served as a "portal for negative energy from beyond," according to Madam X. *Vicki Carter.*

"Just an old secretary desk," Helen told her. "And even before she said, 'I want to see it,' I absolutely knew that it was the desk causing the trouble in the house. I don't know how I knew that it was the source of all that negative energy! But all of a sudden it was absolutely clear to me!"

The desk was old—maybe several hundred years old—and had been given to Helen and her husband by friends in the city soon after they'd bought the beach house. "I really didn't know much about it at that point. We had to furnish this house but we were still living in the city and needed our own furniture to stay where it was. Our friends said we were welcome to the desk. Little did we know."

It was the kind of desk with a fold-down writing surface and lots of cubbies and shelves. There were drawers below, and centered on the front of that fold-down table was a very ornately carved lion. "And that's what Madam X zeroed in on," Helen said. "The lion! She said the desk was a portal and that long ago someone had died or been killed in the room containing the desk. It happened very far away. Maybe even on the East Coast."

Madam X and her helpers smudged the entire house with sage, sprinkled holy water and said prayers. "But of all the parts of the house, she concentrated most of her energy on that lion. That was the portal, she said—an opening between our plane and the other plane. I can't say I quite understand all that, but by the time they left, the house felt calm. Settled. Comfortable."

By now, Helen's husband, Sam, had joined us. "Would you let me take a picture of the desk?" I asked. "Especially of the lion?" And there passed between the two of them one of those been-married-a-long-time looks that those of us who share that status recognize instantly.

"We don't have the desk anymore," Helen said. Then…a long pause. "Sam took it to the dump."

"I thought you wanted to get rid of it," he said. "Not after Madam X had calmed it down," Helen replied. But it was a what's-done-is-done conversation—no regrets, no animosity, just a "case closed" sort of thing.

Channeling Mrs. Kravitz?

"Once they had finished blessing the house," Helen continued, "they had one more chore to complete. "Do you remember the nosy, crotchety neighbor on the old television program *Bewitched*?" she asked. "Mrs. Kravitz?"

Of course I did, and Helen said, "Well, that's my neighbor! And Madam X didn't need to be psychic to see the problems we were having with her. It was just icing on the cake that morning when the Kravitz clone (that's how I think of her) immediately appeared on her deck demanding to know what we were doing. And on my own property too!"

According to Helen, when Madam X was satisfied that she and her helpers had finished up inside the house and that the problem with the desk had been solved, she gathered up her belongings and said she would be back a little later. She had one more thing to do that would settle things down in the neighborhood.

"She came back a little later with six mirrors—smallish ones, about the size of side-view mirrors on cars," Helen said. She attached them on the sides and back of the house. She told me that when someone looked over at our place, their energy would be caught by the mirrors and reflected back to them. Those negative vibes wouldn't penetrate our walls anymore."

"What about the front of the house?" I asked.

"Not a problem," Helen smiled. "Years ago, I purchased a gorgeous piece of Indian fabric. It is called *abhala bharat*, or 'mirror embroidery,' and there are dozens of little mirrors worked into the pattern. Little did I know that the fabrics were said to ward off the evil eye and were traditionally hung in the doorways of people's homes."

Helen had the fabric framed, and as it happened, when they moved into the beach house full time, she found the perfect place to hang it—right in the entry hall facing the front door! "We were covered from that side," she laughed, "and I hadn't even realized it."

"It's been a few years now—lovely, peaceful years. But just lately, that negative energy has started up again," Helen said quietly. "I even tried smudging the house myself! And amazingly, Sam agreed to help! I put every bit of positive thought I could muster into it and tried to channel Madam X, wherever she is. I'm not sure yet whether it worked. And, of course, there's still our difficult neighbor to the north."

Helen was concerned enough to reach out to one of Madam X's former assistants. "She asked me if I had checked on the mirrors lately. And sure enough…every one of them had fallen off the walls. Some were on the ground, damaged or somewhat broken. I've replaced them all now, and we will see. I can only hope the problems in the neighborhood are gone again. When it's calm, it's my favorite place in all the world!"

CHAPTER 9

COPPER WON'T GO INTO THE KITCHEN

In Ocean Park...

> *Look! There in the window! She's waving to us!*
> *—Madam X*

That's one of the last things Madam X said to me," Colleen told me. "I didn't see anyone in the window, waving or not, but that wasn't unusual. Often when I was with Madam X, she would see or hear things that that the rest of us didn't. This time, of course, I knew it was Adelaide Taylor. Adelaide has been here all along."

"Do you want me to ask her to leave?" Madam X asked.

"Heavens no!" Colleen told her. "This is Adelaide's place! She belongs here more than any of us. And besides, Copper likes her. It's just that wicked black cat in the kitchen that he's afraid of."

Copper is Colleen's fifteen-year-old dachshund. He has the run of the place but won't go near the upstairs apartment's kitchen, where, according to Madam X, a cat as big as Copper holds sway. As far as Colleen knows, only Madam X and Copper have met that cat face to face, and despite many attempts to get her to vacate the premises, the cat is having none of it.

Fifteen-year-old Copper loves everyone who visits Adelaide's, including the ghost of Adelaide herself. "Everyone except that cat!" said Colleen Kelly. *Author's collection.*

A REPORT FROM MADAM X

"They're in and out of here like yo-yos," she said. Madam X was, of course, talking about the ghosts that she saw "everywhere" at the Taylor Hotel.

It was a drizzly February afternoon back in 2017, and I was meeting at Adelaide's with Madam X and Colleen Kelly, the new proprietor of the coffee shop. Colleen had asked her friend to come by and assess the situation. She thought I might be interested in hearing the "verdict."

"There was a man who was killed in the street in front of the hotel," Madam X told us. "So far, I haven't learned who he was. I'm not sure he's actually here in the hotel, or if he ever was."

Colleen and I remembered that Jeromy Baker had been working on the porch a while back and found bullet holes and shell casings. "He took the casings home with him," Colleen said, and we all grew quiet. Finally, Colleen asked aloud what we'd all been thinking: "Do you think that's why you haven't heard from that fellow who was killed?" we asked. "Do you think he could have gone home with Jeromy and the casings?" I wonder if she ever found out.

"There were at least four deaths out in the street over the years," Madam X told us. But she had no idea whether they were connected with the hotel. Nor could she yet determine why Copper was cautious about the attic and the upstairs areas. "Even after I gave a blessing in the upstairs kitchen, he wouldn't venture in," she said. ("That was a year or two before the nasty cat was discovered," Colleen added recently.)

"And there's a little girl up in the attic. An indentured servant... there's more work to do here," she told Colleen. "That is, if you want me to...I tell you, they're in and out of here like yo-yos!"

ADELAIDE'S PLACE

The building on Bay Avenue where Colleen insists that Adelaide "belongs" is the old Taylor Hotel. For as long as anyone can recall, the sturdy-looking two-story building has dominated the Bay Avenue streetscape in the heart of Ocean Park. Most folks can't remember it in its heyday, when it truly was a hotel. But over the years, the building has served the community in a multitude of ways and is what many consider a fixture of the Peninsula's North End.

In recent years, the main floor of the building has housed Adelaide's—billed when it opened in 2008 as a "Coffee Shop and Bookstore." Most recently, under the stewardship of Colleen Kelly, the name has been changed to Adelaide's Coffee House and Tapestry Rose Yarn Shop, and it is sometimes known as Adelaide's Coffee and Sweet Shoppe or even Adelaide's Coffee and Yarn Shop. But never mind the name—except the Adelaide's part. Locals know, and visitors soon learn that Adelaide's at the Taylor Hotel on Bay Avenue, no matter how you call it, is *the* gathering place for the north end of the Peninsula. Period.

Work by local artists and writers is for sale there. Knitting classes meet there. Friends rendezvous there for an early breakfast or a leisurely lunch. Adelaide's is where Peninsula folks—visitors as well as residents—congregate for poetry readings, book talks and occasional concerts. On fine days, the action often spills over onto the wide veranda, and even on a blustery winter day, you are likely to see a bundled, hooded figure or two hunkered in an Adirondack chair, deeply engrossed in book or magazine, oblivious of the weather.

Adelaide's was named in honor of Adelaide Stuart Taylor, who, with her husband, William (or "Bill," as he was called), opened Taylor's Hotel as a hotel and boardinghouse in 1887. It soon became a community hub, serving the growing town in myriad ways beyond its commercial hotel and restaurant functions. No doubt the original Adelaide would be pleased that the old hotel has had a twenty-first-century resurgence as the "happening place" of Ocean Park.

In the hotel's heyday, the Taylor family (which included nine children, seven of whom lived to maturity) had their living quarters downstairs. The first floor also contained the kitchen and a large dining room where guests ate meals prepared with vegetables and berries grown in Adelaide's large garden behind the hotel. Rooms were mostly rented by the week or the month during the summer, although there were always a few year-round residents as well. In the 1930s, a week's room and board was ten dollars per person.

"According to family stories, Adelaide had two big wood cookstoves in her kitchen," said her great-great-granddaughter, Paula Cooper, of Ocean Park. "The tops of both stoves would be literally covered with clams or oysters when she was cooking dinner for the hotel patrons. And everything she served was fresh, fresh, fresh!"

When the Ilwaco Railway began its Ilwaco–Nahcotta run in 1889 and access to Peninsula towns grew easier, it soon became apparent that the six

Adelaide Stuart Taylor (1861–1940), Ocean Park's beloved hotel owner, was well known throughout southwestern Washington for her generous community involvement. *Begg Family Photo Collection.*

upstairs guest rooms would not be up to tourist demand. The Taylors lost no time in building a thirty-six-room annex to the east of the hotel. The annex was finally torn down in 1931, with the lumber salvaged and used to build five little cabins across the street from the hotel. Now the cabins, too, are but a memory.

PENINSULA PIONEERS

The Taylors moved to the Ocean Park area in 1886, just three years after the town's beginnings but before it was officially named. They had most recently been residents of Oysterville, where Adelaide worked as a midwife and Bill drove the stagecoach for Lewis Loomis. Bill had also served as

During the 1880s, Bill Taylor drove the stagecoach between Ilwaco and Oysterville. Its twenty-five-mile-route was right along the "weatherbeach" at the Pacific Ocean's edge. *EFA.*

sheriff and assessor for Pacific County in the early 1880s. The Taylors lived on Territory Road, just south of the present-day Oysterville Church.

Like many of the early settlers in the area, Bill had already enjoyed a colorful past. Born in 1845 in Chautauqua County, New York, he had lived in Wisconsin, Minnesota, Kansas and California and worked as a miner, farmer and rail-splitter before arriving in Pacific County in 1876 at the age of thirty-one. Here he met fifteen-year-old Adelaide Stuart and began to think about "settling down."

Unlike her intended, Adelaide was a Pacific County native, born in Bruceport. Her mother, Ophelia, a member of the Quinault tribe, had married Charles Stuart, a white man, which was a practice disapproved of by the Quinaults at that time. Therefore, Adelaide's family had moved to the Columbia River area, where the Chinook tribe held no such taboos against intermarriage.

Longtime Ocean Park resident Adelle Beechey remembered Adelaide as "a tiny little woman, maybe four feet nine or ten," who was still running the hotel in 1936 when Adelle moved to town. "Her daughter, Mary, was about my age. We had gone to school together in Ilwaco," Adelle said.

According to some reports, Adelaide and Bill Taylor had moved to the area that would become Ocean Park in an effort to get away from the rowdy, boomtown atmosphere of Oysterville five miles to the north. Others surmised that Taylor's job as a stagecoach driver had given him an insider's understanding of the tourist trade that Loomis's new railroad would bring to the area. The Ocean Park train depot would be built in 1889 just a short distance from the Taylors' new Ocean Park home.

FIRST, A RESTAURANT

They soon established a large vegetable garden—a garden that would continue to supply produce for the Taylor family and their hotel patrons for nearly fifty years. Perhaps their bountiful garden was in part responsible for the Taylors' first business venture in Ocean Park: a restaurant. Undoubtedly, it was the first commercial eating establishment in the three-year-old settlement. Known familiarly as the "Methodist Camp Ground," the 250-acre "resort" was still owned and managed by the Ocean Park Camp Meeting Association of the Methodist Episcopal Church in Portland.

By the time the resort was named "Ocean Park" in 1888, the association was beginning to allow "outsiders" to purchase property. The record is silent

First the Taylors' restaurant (mid-1880s) and then the Methodists' first chapel (mid-1890s), this building, many times renovated, still stands at Bay and Melrose in Ocean Park. *PCHS.*

on whether the Taylors were members of the association when they bought the property for their restaurant and, a year later, for their hotel. However, once the Taylor Hotel was up and running, they sold the restaurant, which then became the first Methodist Chapel in Ocean Park. After William Taylor died in 1919, Adelaide remarried. She continued to run the hotel until well into the 1930s, and it was not until her death in 1940 that the Taylor Hotel was sold and passed out of the family.

Throughout its fifty-year history, the building often served as headquarters for important community functions, from providing housing for shipwrecked sailors to hosting fundraising activities for local and regional projects. By the 1920s, when automobiles were becoming increasingly popular, local residents began putting their efforts into the establishment of roads to "the outside." In 1925, the Taylor Hotel played its part by hosting fundraisers to benefit construction of the K.M. highway from Longview to Long Beach—the road now known as Washington State Route 4.

The first streetlights in Ocean Park were also financed largely through proceeds from card parties held at the Taylor Hotel—"Admission 50 cents per person, 75 cents per couple; refreshments included" said the announcements.

Perhaps the biggest changes witnessed by the hotel and its owners over the years were the advances in transportation. When the Taylors first established their business in 1887, guests arrived by the Loomis Stagecoach, which traveled on the hard sands of the ocean beach from Ilwaco to Oysterville. It is easy to speculate that Bill and Adelaide located their hotel close to the beach with that stagecoach transport in mind. Bill undoubtedly "delivered" many a passenger to the Methodist Resort during his final years as a driver and could imagine the convenience of a hotel just steps away from the stage stop.

By the time Adelaide and Bill had opened their small restaurant, the narrow-gauge railroad was the talk of the Peninsula. Locating their hotel near the beach but also only a few blocks from the train depot was probably no accident. The Taylors were canny that way. Within three years, travelers were coming north from Ilwaco in the relative comfort of the train, with the final destination for numerous passengers being Ocean Park.

Many are the stories of the crowds that gathered at the Ocean Park Depot on summer weekends awaiting the arrival of the Saturday evening "Papa Train"—so called because of the numbers of men who came from Portland each week to join their vacationing families at the beach. A "baggage man" would meet the train with his horse and wagon, load up all the luggage and

A SHIPWRECKED SAILOR'S HAVEN

The area of the Pacific Ocean that lies just beyond the doorstep of the Taylor Hotel is called the "Graveyard of the Pacific." There, in the two-hundred-mile stretch north and south from the Columbia River's mouth, turbulent seas and tidal rips, rocky reefs and shorelines have claimed more than two thousand ships and seven hundred lives since 1792, the year Captain Robert Gray threaded his way into the great river of the west. Although major wrecks have declined since the introduction of modern aids to navigation in the 1920s, several lives are still lost there annually. Three enduring stories are told about the Taylor Hotel's role in early shipwrecks.

The first involves William "Willie" Begg, forebear of several Peninsula residents. Willie arrived "all of a sudden" on the three-masted barque *Glenmorag* of Glasgow that grounded near Ocean Park on March 19, 1896. While

When thick fog obscured the grounded *Glenmorag* from shore in 1896, young crewman Willie Begg managed to get to the Taylor Hotel for help. *PCHS.*

Sometimes called a "ghost ship," the *Solano* has disappeared and reappeared several times in the shifting sands north of Ocean Park since 1907. *EFA.*

attempting to escape the wreck, two of the twenty-seven seamen were killed and several injured, including Willie. Nevertheless, he was the one who made it to the Taylor Hotel to sound the alarm. According to some accounts, it was young Maud Taylor, daughter of the hotel proprietors, who answered the door and removed nineteen-year-old Willie's shoes and fetched warm blankets for him.

For the next two years, Willie lived aboard the ship, guarding it for the owners. When final attempts to refloat it failed, the ship was dismantled; its remains were abandoned, and it was left to be consumed by the ever-accreting sands. Not long afterward, in true fairy tale fashion, Willie Begg and Maud Taylor married and settled in Ocean Park, where they lived a long and satisfying life.

Eleven years later, on February 5, 1907, the four-masted schooner *Solano* was grounded about four miles north of Ocean Park. All seamen aboard the ship at the time of its grounding were saved by the North Beach Life-Saving Station crew within a short time after the distress signal had been set off.

All hands aboard the *Alice* reached shore safely, their ship's boats having made a successful run through the high surf a mile north of Ocean Park. *EFA*.

Willie Taylor, one of the sons of Adelaide and Bill Taylor, fell heir to a dog that came in on the *Solano* and named him for the ship. Just two years later, in the icy early morning hours of January 15, 1909, the graceful French sailing ship *Alice* ran aground north of Ocean Park. It was Willie Taylor's dog, Solano, that discovered the ship in the surf and came barking to her master.

Young Willie Taylor then spread the news of the wreck and alerted the lifesaving station at Klipsan Beach. The twenty-four-man crew were all saved, although the ship was a total loss. Its 2,200-ton cargo of cement had immediately catalyzed into hard packets from the salt water. Plans for its salvage were not even considered.

The crew of the ship stayed at the Taylor Hotel until they could be transported to Portland and, from there, home to France.* Able-bodied seaman Louis DeReugemond wrote home, "We've been living royally here on shore and feel fine, but it seems too bad to see that fine steel packet out there digging her own grave in the sand." During their stay, local sixteen-year-old Beulah Slingerland (Wickberg)

---

* In an unexpected postscript to the *Alice*'s story, in 2019 Isabelle le Corguillé came from her home in France to pay a visit to the Taylor Hotel. As a nineteen-year-old sailor, her grand-père Jean-Marie Dauvé had been among the shipwrecked crew of the *Alice*, and Isabelle had grown up hearing his stories of his stay in faraway Ocean Park. She came to see it for herself.

In January 1909, the *Alice* crew posed with Taylor family members in front of the Taylor Hotel. At left, front are Willie Taylor and his heroic dog, Solano. *EFA*.

(1893–1995) sometimes played the piano for the young sailors. Throughout her long life, she remembered those evenings with fondness and remarked wistfully, "The language of music is international."

deliver it to the hotel and to various summer homes and boardinghouses. (And on a "small world" note typical of the communities on the Long Beach Peninsula, the baggage delivery man for years was the aforementioned Adelle Beechey's father-in-law!)

Both William David Taylor (1845–1919) and Adelaide Stuart Taylor (1861–1940) are buried at the Ocean Park Cemetery, less than a mile from their esteemed hotel. Most people familiar with Adelaide's story, however, believe that she has never really left her beloved establishment and are more than ready to believe that she is upstairs keeping an eye on things, as she did for most of her long life. "We like having her up there," said Colleen. "Even Copper seems to get along fine with her. It's just that nasty cat in the kitchen he has trouble with."

CHAPTER 10
WHERE THE OLD ILWACO HOSPITAL USED TO BE

In Ilwaco...

Since the time of its construction in 1938, the "Old Ilwaco Hospital" has been refurbished, renovated, reconstructed and, finally, repurposed. Through all its configurations, the rumors about the ghosts in the structure on the hillside north of Ilwaco have persisted. Over the years, the building's employees and visitors have reported hearing "noises": footsteps on the stairs, furniture being moved around in the attic, clanking sounds in the area that served as the hospital's morgue—although where that was, exactly, seems to vary with each telling. And there were other manifestations as well.

The original building, half the size that it would eventually be, was a $17,000 project, jointly funded by an $8,000 Works Progress Administration (WPA) grant and by the State of Washington, Pacific County, the Town of Ilwaco and the Peninsula community. "It is part of a movement to put men to work and get orders for materials following as rapidly as possible," wrote Frank Turner in his *Tribune* column, "From Auld Lang Syne."

Construction was by Ilwaco contractor Brumbaugh and the Petit brothers, also of Ilwaco. Situated south of Black Lake, the building was surrounded by an unpaved parking lot covered with rocks and gravel and usually, in the rainy Northwest climate, hosting large rain ponds. Behind it was a swamp forest.

Although the building that now houses the Ilwaco Timberland Library is still known as "the Old Ilwaco Hospital," it was the second, not the

Shown here in 1950, the "Old Ilwaco Hospital" was constructed with WPA funds in 1938 and was soon serving communities far beyond the Peninsula. *SPP.*

Most recently a bed-and-breakfast establishment, the lovely Henry Freeborough home in Seaview served as the Peninsula's first hospital from 1931 to 1938. *Author's collection.*

first, hospital on the Peninsula. Prior to its construction in 1938, there had been a hospital in Seaview on the corner of Pacific Way and "L" Place—the very first Ocean Beach Hospital.

A headline in the July 3, 1931 issue of the *Chinook Observer* announced "Ocean Beach Hospital Officially Open—Silver Tea Draws Many to Open House at Seaview Institution." The upscale opening celebration honored the new establishment and its most unconventional beginnings. This first Ocean Beach Hospital was started by Dr. David Strang, who was new to the Peninsula, and by a nurse from Astoria named Mrs. Loftgren, who later admitted that she was "mainly looking for adventure in the Peninsula's primitive surroundings."

I was working for CCAP* in the bottom of the old hospital in Ilwaco in 2016. Sometimes we would smell rotting flesh. I swear! It was so disgusting I almost got sick. I had to cover my face just to get out of the building.

—Jerri Hawks, 2020

Dr. Strang felt strongly that the Peninsula needed a hospital closer in proximity than the only two in the region—in South Bend and in Astoria. After all, those sick enough to require hospitalization were often too ill to travel. So, the good doctor began a fundraising campaign. "To all persons donating as much as $25 in support, he will credit a week's use of the hospital," announced the April 20, 1929 issue of the *North Beach Tribune*. His hope was to raise enough for a small, six-bed facility.

As it turned out, the Great Depression and the hard times that followed interfered with Dr. Strang's plans. However, in May 1931 *The Tribune* reported the surprising news that Mr. and Mrs. Henry Freeborough had sold their large Seaview home to Mrs. Della Loftgren, who would convert it into a hospital! Mrs. Loftgren was eminently qualified, having managed the Corvallis, Oregon hospital; having served as matron in charge of Astoria's Columbia Hospital; and having been a member of the Oregon State Hospital Board.

So favorably did the Freeboroughs feel about having a hospital at the beach, they had happily moved into a small house nearby and even supplied milk to the facility from their family cow. Dr. and Mrs. Strang lived in the new hospital, with Mrs. S. helping with almost everything, including administering anesthetic ether. By July 1931, the *Observer* was reporting the

---

* The Coastal Community Action Program (CCAP) provides in-home care services for the disabled and seniors.

success of the first surgical procedure at the new Ocean Beach Hospital: the removal of Mrs. Frank Lyniff's abscessed appendix.

The facility included a large room for a ward where old folks with or without significant illness were kept and a large number of small rooms where more critical patients were treated. Mrs. Loftgren prepared meals in the small kitchen and did laundry on the back porch, where there was a washing machine for all hospital materials. Sterilization was accomplished by soaking instruments in a large pan of antiseptic liquid.

Except for the provision for doing blood counts, there was no laboratory, nor was there any X-ray capability. Anesthesia was administered by Mrs. Loftgren via a pinhole in the cap of a can of ether dripping onto some cotton wool beneath a wire mask—later known as "rag and can" anesthesia by critics, but according to Dr. John Campiche, who joined the hospital staff in 1953, "It was, in fact, very safe albeit unpleasant." After surgery, the patient was carried by the nurse and doctor on a stretcher back to his or her room upstairs. Nurse Alice Christianson drove the ambulance, which was used not only to take patients to the hospital but also to take them home, since cars were still few and far between on the Peninsula.

Decades later, in August 2000, Campiche said of Dr. Strang, "He belonged to a prior generation of tireless doctors…doctors who diagnosed ailments and disease by the appearance, history and physical findings at bedside rather than, as now, with laboratory, X-ray, ultrasound and scanner electronics. There was neither legal liability nor lawsuits; patients took their chances and accepted whatever their fates."

Once the Ilwaco Hospital was up and running, the Seaview property reverted to private ownership. For years, it belonged to Ray Provo Sr. and family and, in recent years, has served as a bed-and-breakfast establishment. Perhaps not surprisingly, there have been periodic reports of "unexplained happenings" in the old building.

"It wasn't much by urban standards," Dr. Campiche said of the Ilwaco Hospital in a 2000 reminiscence for the *Chinook Observer*. "It didn't even look like a hospital, but it was a vast improvement over the Freeborough House conversion. The building comprised what is now the south part of the

After a while we didn't pay any attention anymore. We knew those footsteps didn't belong to anyone— not to anyone we could see, anyway.

—Betty Newell, Pacific Aging Council Endeavors (PACE), 1985

THEY WERE ALL WEARING WHITE

In 2008, when Mr. and Mrs. Robert Chamberlain of Northwest Paranormal Investigations came to look into possible ghost activities at the old Ocean Beach Hospital in Ilwaco, they knew nothing of the historic Seaview hospital site. After all, it had been seventy years since the building had served in a medical capacity, and few people remembered that it had even existed. When their hosts mentioned the site of the Peninsula's first hospital, the Chamberlains asked to go there immediately.

They headed first to the attic, where they encountered a little girl in a long white dress—an apparition, they were to learn, that had been reported many times over the years. Back downstairs and out in the garden, they watched a group of people, also in white, playing croquet. They placed the year at 1911, some twenty years prior to the hospital's beginnings—indeed, about the time the Freeboroughs had built there.

According to the grandson of the Freeboroughs, his grandparents had told him that, in the past, there had been croquet games on the lawn on Sunday mornings. Although Chamberlain did feel "the presence of children" in one of the rooms, no further information was forthcoming about the little girl in the long white dress.

Ilwaco library and the PACE* Center." That was in 2000, nine years before the building, now called the Ilwaco Community Center, had been enlarged and improved once again.

Soon after its 1938 construction, in addition to the Peninsula, the Ilwaco Hospital was serving Grays River, Deep River, Naselle and Chinook, as well as parts of Bay Center. By the late 1940s, in deference to those patients coming from far beyond Ilwaco, the hospital had changed its name to Ocean Beach Hospital.

According to those who worked with him, Dr. David Strang was not one to be put aside by inconveniences, having never known anything else. He was a true pioneer doctor and a good one. He had no backup, surgical assistants,

---

* Pacific Aging Council Endeavors (PACE), until 2009, was an organization that provided nutrition programs for seniors and the disabled on the Long Beach Peninsula.

technicians or other doctors. "During World War II, Dr. Strang returned from retirement to cover the Peninsula," Dr. Campiche said of him. "He was already an old man, but effective nevertheless."

Frequent Trauma and Death

Dr. Campiche had arrived on the Peninsula fresh from an internship and residence in Grand Rapids, Michigan. "A major difference in the practice of medicine here… was that the hospital did not play a dominant role in everyday medical care. Even in the East, hospital care had not yet become as completely dependent upon laboratory facilities. The doctor's office and house calls were still the setting for most medical care. Major surgery, serious illness and especially major injury were what took patients to the hospital."

We would hear someone walking around in the building. I would run up the stairs as fast as I could to try and catch them, but when I got upstairs there was no one. The building was empty. This happened about four different times.

—J.H., 2020

Injuries from on-the-job accidents were frequent in those days. The major industries in the area were fishing, farming and logging but, according to Dr. Campiche, "without any regulation to prevent injury in these dangerous occupations. At that time, Pacific County was like a war zone: trauma and death were brutal and frequent." To further complicate matters, there would be no bridge access across the Columbia until 1966, so there was no effective relief from the larger medical community of Astoria, Oregon.

"There were few of the treatment modalities common today such as antibiotics or intravenous fluid support. Surgery included the common surgical operations of the day…gall bladder removals, hysterectomies, various gynecological procedures, caesarean sections and the treatments of the many fractures and injuries. One did the best one could with tender loving care, morphine, warmth and hope; yet the best was quite good at that," Campiche wrote. "The most common threatening illnesses of those days were bacterial pneumonia, diabetic coma, strokes and heart failure. One difference was that there were no means of prolonging life, advisable or not, so that when treatment failed, one was done and that was that."

"Furthermore," Campiche continued, "each summer we were burdened with an increasing number of tourists, thousands on big holidays. We would all heave a collective sigh of relief when Labor Day came and Long Beach boarded up its windows and shut down. I thought of the tourists as being like lemmings who mysteriously run in great flocks down to the sea and jump off the cliffs to their doom: they did crazy things they would never do at home."

In one corner of the kitchen, things would fall out of the cupboards, and hanging utensils would swing for no apparent reason. And it got to where we were so freaked out that neither of us would take out the garbage by ourselves.

—J.H., 2020

ROOM AND BOARD FOR NURSES

On the Ilwaco Hospital's main floor were eight patient beds and a nursery area with three cribs. Several additional beds, cots and stretchers could be pressed into service if needed. Newborns were placed in padded laundry baskets unless families supplied their own cribs. Located in the basement was the furnace, storage, a kitchen, a makeshift emergency room, vegetable storage bins and space for the X-ray machine. Above, in the attic, were additional storage areas and rooms for nurses, who by 1940 received fifty-five dollars per month plus board and room.

Amenities were meager by today's standards. There was no laboratory or autoclave sterilizer. Instruments were sterilized in a pressure cooker on the kitchen stove. According to Dr. Campiche, "The X-ray machine purchased by Dr. Strang must have been the second model after Roentgen invented the device. It had an open unshielded tube that sprayed X-rays in all directions that passed on or through everything except its target, the photographic plate!"

In 1946, after World War II, Dr. Lewis C. Neace, a native of Eastern Washington, returned from years in army MASH units in the Pacific and took up practice on the Peninsula, replacing Dr. Strang and opening an office first in a motel in Long Beach and, later, above the drugstore in Ilwaco. He added much equipment to the little hospital, including, importantly, an autoclave for sterilization and an upgrade in the X-ray machine housed in the basement.

Dr. Neace (1909–2004) practiced medicine for fifty-one of his ninety-five years, mostly on the Peninsula. He had been in practice on the Peninsula for seven or eight years when Dr. John Campiche joined him at the Ilwaco Hospital. "He was probably the best clinician I ever knew," Campiche said

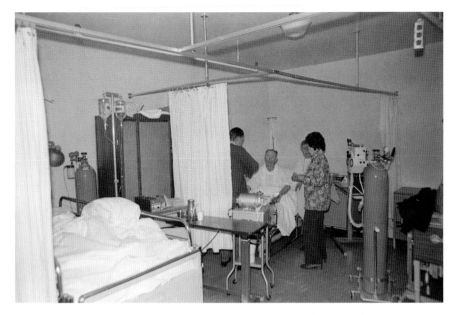

There were two- and four-patient wards and one private room, for a capacity of twenty beds at the time of this picture in 1950. *SPP.*

of him years later. "He was an old-fashioned type of doctor and a bedside expert. He didn't rely on technology as much as on physical examinations and patient history and his knowledge of medicine."

Campiche went on to say, "He knew more about trauma treatment than anyone I ever knew. He never saw anyone smashed up that he didn't think could be fixed. He had a lot of knowledge of all the diseases that existed and how they manifested themselves. I saw him do things in surgery that were simply laudable and that took a lot of courage and ability."

By 1940, there was a primitive X-ray machine, but without a technician. There was no anesthesia equipment, incubator for premature babies, fracture table, electrocardiograph or dictating machines, to name a few of the amenities that big-city hospitals might have had available. Gradually, though, progress was made. Dr. Campiche's training in anesthesiology in combination with a good anesthesia machine increased the possibilities for safe surgeries. The first two laboratory technicians helped increase the hospital's bottom line. Within a few years, Congress

Sometimes, looking through the window, I saw a man over there holding a baby. Right over there! In the area that was the maternity ward.

—Kathy White, librarian, 2005

Top: As far as is known, no citations were issued for this most unusual accident. *SPP.*

Bottom: Perhaps it was thought that on the Peninsula, where "everybody knows everybody," the ribbing Ms. Graham was sure to encounter would be punishment enough. *SPP.*

Thus far, there is no evidence that there was any paranormal activity connected with Letha Graham's decidedly abnormal entrance into the Old Ilwaco Hospital in the early 1970s. Nor is there any information as to how it happened that the Dodge Charger she was driving took her straight into the building without benefit of even a pause at the admitting desk. Ms. Graham, who was the proprietor of the New Seara Convalescent Home in Long Beach, stepped out of the automobile unscathed, while various Ilwaco emergency crews puzzled over the unusual occurrence. Even now, years later, the historic record is silent on the matter.

had passed a law that gave hospitals, nursing homes and other health facilities grants and loans for construction and modernization.

In 1958, the first addition costing $135,000 was built. It included two parallel extensions to the north. The extension on the parking lot contained wards and a private room; the other, in the back, contained the operating room, delivery room, preparation room and scrub room.

Between them was a laboratory and X-ray facility. As for the stairway leading up, "It led to recovery, not heaven," was the oft-quoted quip by Dr. Lewis Neace.

Not State of the Art

Even with the upgrades, however, by the mid-'60s, the need for a new and modern hospital had become apparent. However, no longer did doctors and the community have the exclusive right to determine what a new facility should be. The Washington State Department of Health was, by now, overseer of medical and hospital care and agent for the federal Health and Human Services authority. When all was said and done, the new hospital at a cost of $2.5 million was, according to the front-line healthcare professionals, "posterity's stepchild, born into the bad times of awesomely increased hospital costs and plagued with problems from the start." It opened in 1976.

So far, there are no reports of ghost activity at the present-day Ocean Beach Hospital, situated just two blocks north of the old hospital. *OBHMC.*

Meanwhile, the "old hospital building," now the Ilwaco Community Center, had problems of its own. Ghosts! The new hospital on the hill had barely opened when the reports about strange goings-on in the old facility began. People walking up and down the stairs, furniture being moved around in the attic, unsavory smells and, occasionally, a person (perhaps a visitor) outside looking in were all reported—some repeatedly over the years.

A couple of times I heard the upstairs piano playing and I went up to check. The Senior Center was closed and no one was playing the piano.

—J.H., 2020

Accounts have come from all parts of the Ilwaco Community Center—from the various county agencies that have been housed there and from the staff of the Timberland Ilwaco Library, which occupies the northern portion of the building. Told by visitors and employees, the experiences are often similar, even though they have happened years apart. Workers continue to report hearing voices in the hallway, and occasionally the doorbell rings even though no one is there.

Now and then, a bit of fantasy is thrown in as well. Reports of "the morgue" and the "the maternity ward" were routinely scoffed at by the "old guard"—those nurses and staff members who had worked in the old hospital. "What morgue? We didn't have a morgue!…Maternity ward, indeed! That would be the room to which the pregnant mom was assigned. We didn't have the population for an entire maternity ward!"

THE INVESTIGATORS ARRIVE

Still, by 2003, there had been enough reports to merit attention by the Northwest Paranormal Investigations, an Oregon-based organization with chapters in Portland, St. Helens, Clackamas County, Beaverton and Oakland, Oregon. The group came to the Peninsula in force—twelve members, armed with tools of their trade—the weekend of March 15–16, 2003. They came purposely at that time in order to be here on March 17, which was a full moon. "Activity is stronger then," said Robert Chamberlain, founder and president of the organization.

They brought with them still and video cameras, thermometers, motion detectors and an electromagnetic field detector. They visited both the site of the first Peninsula hospital in Seaview as well as the site of the Old Ilwaco Hospital. At the conclusion of their visit, the investigators

Haunted or not, I love it here. My conclusion is we're not supposed to know everything.

—Kristine Pointer, Ilwaco Library, 2005

declared both sites "active," which indicates to Chamberlain that "there's a lot going on."

"Our goal is to see an apparition," Chamberlain said, "but usually we see an orb of electromagnetic energy." The orbs can be seen in photographs of areas where a presence has been detected. Orbs and presences had been felt at both old hospital sites, but only in Seaview had an apparition appeared. But then, just before leaving Ilwaco, investigators were outside, at the east windows of the library. They said they saw an apparition of a man holding a baby. That portion of the library had been the maternity ward when the hospital occupied the building…or so they had been told.

Their findings did not come as a surprise to many community members, especially those who have worked in and around the old hospital building.

ILWACO COMMUNITY BUILDING

The structure underwent major renovation beginning in March 2008, and although it is now officially the Ilwaco Community Building, it is still called the "Old Ilwaco Hospital" with affection. One almost feels as though the strange stories are part of the charm of the old building, and only when it is associated with its beginnings as a hospital do the stories have that shivery feeling that accompanies all good ghost stories.

Meanwhile, up the hill, the "new" Ocean Beach Hospital continues to refine and upgrade its spaces and continues to provide up-to-date services to the communities of the Long Beach Peninsula and surrounding areas. Whether or not the facility is attracting its own cadre of ghosts is yet to be determined. So far, there are no reports of unusual activity or unexplained phenomena there. Perhaps it's only a matter of time.

BIBLIOGRAPHY

Books

Baker, Reverend J.C. *Baptist History of the North Pacific Coast*. Philadelphia, PA: Baptist Publication Society, 1912.

Davis, Charlotte. *They Remembered, Book IV*. Long Beach, WA: Midway Printery, 1994.

Davis, Charlotte, and Edgar Davis. *They Remembered, Books I, II, III*. Ilwaco, WA: Pacific Printing, 1981–92.

Duer, Douglas. *Empires of the Turning Tide*. National Park Service, U.S. Department of the Interior. Washington, D.C.: Government Printing Office, 2016.

Feagans, Raymond. *The Railroad that Ran by the Tide*. Berkeley, CA: Howell North Books, 1972.

Gibbs, James A. *Pacific Graveyard*. Portland, OR: Binfords & Mort, 1973.

Hawthorne, Julian. *History of Washington*. Vols. 1 and 2. New York: American Historical Publishing Company, 1893.

Hazeltine, Jean. *Willapa Bay, Its Historical and Regional Geography*. South Bend, WA: South Bend Journal, 1956.

History of Pacific Northwest Oregon and Washington. Vols. 1 and 2. Portland, OR: North Pacific History Company, 1889.

Ilwaco's Early Finns Pacific County, Washington. Portland, OR: Finnish American Historical Society, January 1992.

Lemeshko, Michael. *The Cantankerous Farmer vs. The Ilwaco Railway & Navigation Company and the Rest of His Neighbors on the Long Beach Peninsula*. Bothell, WA: Cantankerous Books, 2010.

Lloyd, Nancy. *Observing Our Peninsula's Past*. Vols. 1 and 2. Long Beach. WA: Chinook Observer, 2003 and 2006.

McDonald, Lucile. *Coast Country: A History of Southwest Washington*. Portland, OR: Binfords & Mort, Publishers, 1966.

Oesting, Marie. *Oysterville Cemetery Sketches*. Ocean Park, WA, 1988.

Williams, John G. *Johnny Stories, Scenes from My Boyhood in Old Ilwaco*. Ilwaco, WA: Pacific Printing Company, 1987.

Magazines

Sou'wester, Quarterly Magazine of the Pacific County Historical Society 6, no. 3 (Fall 1971); 9, no. 2 (Summer 1974); 10, no. 4 (Winter 1975); 16, no. 4 (Winter 1981); 27, no. 2 (Summer 1992); 36, no. 3 (Fall 2001); 60–61, nos. 4/1 (Winter/Spring/Summer/Fall 2005–6); nos. 2–3 (Summer/Fall 2011); and nos. 1–4 (Spring/Summer/Fall/Winter 2014).

Newspapers

Chinook Observer, various issues.

Ilwaco Tribune/North Beach Tribune/The Tribune (various issues with titles changing over the years).

Los Angeles Herald, August 21, 1897.

Los Angeles Times, December 23, 1894.

Morning Astorian, July 24, 1904.

North Pacific Union Gleaner, May 31, 1938.

Oregon Daily Journal, September 3, 1910.

Seattle Daily Times, November 28, 1911.

South Bend Journal, various issues.

St. Louis Post Dispatch, June 23, 1924.

Sunday Oregonian, July 22, 1906.

Official Records

Department of the Interior, U.S. Board on Geographic Names, 1950.

National Register of Historic Places, Office of Archaeology and Historic Preservation, Washington, D.C., 1976.

Oysterville Baptist Church Records, 1892–1980, Espy Family Archive, Oysterville and Tacoma.

Oysterville Cemetery Association, "Old Linen Map," circa 1905.

"Statutes of the Territory of Washington 1854," Olympia, Washington, 1855.

U.S. Federal Census, Pacific County, Washington, 1860.

Washington State Legislature Revised Code of Washington.

Websites and Archives

Ancestry.com.

Espy Family Archives. Washington State Historical Society Research Center, Tacoma, Washington.

INDEX

ABOUT THE AUTHOR

 It stands to reason that I have a particular affection for ghosts," laughs author/historian Sydney Stevens. "I'm among the oldest residents of our little village of Oysterville—the town my great-grandfather cofounded in 1854 and where my family has had a presence since the beginning. Nowadays, I have more friends and relatives in our cemetery than there are people living in our community!" Sydney and her husband, Nyel, live in the house that was once the parsonage for the historic Oysterville Church. "Three generations have shared this house with Mrs. Crouch—the ghostly wife of the very first minister who lived here and preached across the street. Her story prompted *Ghost Stories of the Long Beach Peninsula*. The lingering questions about her unrighteous husband led to yet another book of ghost stories—this one!"